Always
in
Fashion

Always in Fashion

FROM CLERK TO CEO—
LESSONS FOR SUCCESS
IN BUSINESS AND IN LIFE

MARK WEBER

New York Chicago San Francisco Athens London Madrid
Mexico City Milan New Delhi Singapore Sydney Toronto

1 2 3 4 5 6 7 8 9 0   DOC/DOC   1 2 0 9 8 7 6 5 4

ISBN   978-0-07-184939-5
MHID   0-07-184939-4

e-ISBN   978-0-07-184940-1
e-MHID   0-07-184940-8

Library of Congress Cataloging-in-Publication Data

Weber, Mark
    Always in fashion : from clerk to CEO : lessons for success in business and in life / Mark Weber. — 1 Edition.
        pages cm
    ISBN 978-0-07-184939-5 (hardback : alk paper) — ISBN 0-07-184939-4 (alk. paper) 1. Success in business. 2. Self-realization. 3. Career development. I. Title.
HF5386.W334 2015
650.1—dc23
                                                            2014036454

Only in America

CONTENTS

INTERMISSION
The Search

ACT II
The Best Is Yet to Come

ACT III
Weber's World

PREFACE

Human Nature

Success has many fathers;
failure is an orphan.

There is an ancient Japanese story that three samurai each told from their individual perspectives. There was a great battle. The shogun was saved by the samurai, yet only one could have saved him; the others were not mentioned.

My wife and I went to Egypt, where we took a cruise down the Nile. It was fascinating, to say the least. Although I remember the pyramids and Sphinx, which I toured on an Arabian horse, I remember one story even more clearly.

After touring all the ancient monuments, one astute tourist asked a question of the tour guide: "Egypt has a 3,000-year history, but it looks like all the surviving monuments and temples have the name of the same pharaoh. Why is that?"

The guide smiled and said, "That's human nature. Each successive pharaoh had the prior pharaoh's name sandblasted off everything and replaced with his own name."

With this as a background, I must state that this book is being written with the knowledge that my name has been sandblasted from the events, accomplishments, and plaques in my prior business lives. It's human nature to re-create or recredit accomplishments in the absence of the samurai, the pharaoh, or in this case the executive.

I am sure many people from my former life will be surprised to read that I existed or that many of the accomplishments were actually mine. Nonetheless, these stories or insights are true, and they are mine. As I often say, there are no flukes in business. You can't have a consistent or important career without earning it. In my case, my journey from clerk to CEO are the facts, and I earned my way there at PVH.

Act II at LVMH is something I talk about in detail. I apply many of the principles to governing in the business world. These ideas and principles have served me well. This is currently my eighth year in an originally three-year term.

I would like to think there are lessons to be learned, and maybe, just maybe, you will enjoy my story and career to date.

MARK WEBER

INTRODUCTION

Work Is Work If It's Work

So far, I have had a fantastic career. I started out with nothing—no experience and no career guidance—and became CEO of one of the most prestigious men's companies in the world and then the CEO North America of arguably the finest luxury company in the world.

The fact that you've picked up this book and started reading means that you're at least a little interested in knowing more about the fashion industry and how to succeed in it. You're probably even more interested in finding out what you can learn from my experiences that will help you in your own career. If you work in the fashion, retail, or luxury-goods industries or want to, I believe this book will help you in ways you never thought possible. If you work in any other industry, this book can help you because much of what I've accomplished, achieved, and learned over the course of my career applies to anyone working anywhere.

This book grew out of the desire to help people who may be in the same situation I was in when I started out. I knew no one. I had no connections. I had no advisors. I had no idea how to get started in a career. I only knew I wanted to. I am first and foremost a creative person. I learned early on, however, that creativity without business knowledge and skills is limiting. And I was willing to work hard, very hard.

I believe the story of my career and the experiences I've had—good and bad, successes and failures—will be helpful to other people, and not only people working in the fashion or retail industry but people working in any industry. I've learned everything I could about the workings of the fashion business—and business in general. I have gained a wealth of knowledge and learned lessons that I think are interesting and inspirational and can help people learn and grow. I've lectured to students from many walks of life, and whenever I do, the majority of questions I'm confronted with and asked to relate to take the following form: How did you get where you are? How did you become successful? What were the key elements of getting ahead? These questions come not only from young people who are just starting out but also from senior executives in other businesses and industries. As we all know, in today's economy, there are many people who are out of work or in jobs they're unhappy with or who don't have the careers they want. I've been asked so often about my success that I've started to feel more like an employment recruiter than a business manager: so many people seek me out and ask for help.

This book provides guidance on problems that many people in many industries face. Simply put, if you love what you're doing, you're going to love your career. It's very important to find something you can enjoy doing every day. If you don't, it will be work. You'll be miserable, and you'll suffer through each day. If you really want to get ahead, you have to find your niche, something you really are passionate about; then you'll never complain, you'll never feel work is drudgery, and you'll be moving in the right direction. Your work won't be perfect (it never is), but you will be fighting through the politics and people and focusing on learning and performing, not on the drudgery or misery of misspent time.

I realized right away that I enjoyed the world of fashion, and everything I did grew from this feeling in my heart that I was doing something I wanted to do and could be good at and excel in. People need to find their calling. Maybe you won't find it right away, but if you really want to have a chance to be successful, I advise you to look for something you're going to enjoy and not be afraid to change direction if you don't. I truly believe that one of the most important factors— maybe the most important factor—in being successful is finding something you want to do.

Some of you reading this book may think, That's easy for you to say: you found what you love right away. Some of you may feel you don't have any idea what you want to do with your lives. I understand that, but I believe that if you really think about it, you may already know in your heart of hearts what you want to do. Or you may learn what it is from a teacher or someone else in your life: a friend, a partner, a family member. You may not realize it in your first job or your second job, but I believe you'll know at some point during the course of your life. I ended up in fashion by accident. I had no idea what I wanted to do when I graduated from college. Then, when I started working at my first job, it just felt right. That's what happened to me, and I believe it can happen to you, too. I believe there are lessons from my career that can help others have the kinds of careers they want to have. And I'm willing to share my story, mistakes and all, to provide that help.

I've organized this book into four parts. Act I describes how I got started in the fashion business, the hurdles I overcame, and the lessons I learned as I worked my way up from an entry-level position as an assistant designer to the CEO of the largest shirt company in the world.

Then I was fired, and I had to learn how to find a job after working for a single company for 33 years. The Intermission reveals how I applied myself to the search for a new position. Even though I could easily have retired and never worked another day in my life, I didn't want to do that. As too many people today know, looking for work when you're older is no picnic—not even if you've been a CEO. But I persevered, and I found an even more exciting position at Donna Karan International and LVMH.

Act II describes the challenges I faced when I began the second phase of my career at DKI. The brand was bigger than the business, and my mission was to meet the company's financial goals. To do that, I needed to build the brand, find new ways to market it, and establish some basic rules and procedures to ensure that the company ran smoothly. Along the way, I learned about the women's fashion business and global business, and I share those lessons here.

Act III provides a variety of other ideas and principles that I think are helpful to anyone working in any capacity today. Some of this is specific to the fashion industry, but all of it is useful for anyone who wants to succeed in any business. I hope you agree, and I wish you good luck in your career. But remember, luck will take you only so far: the rest is up to you.

ACT I

In the Beginning

1

I Wasn't Supposed to Have This Career

I didn't have any direction when I was starting out in my career, and I didn't have anyone to advise me. I had amazing, wonderful parents: I was loved and nurtured, and they taught me right from wrong, black from white, with no gray. They were good providers with excellent moral standards, and they were absolutely my role models in life. I would not trade my childhood for anything. However, neither of my parents went to college. My father was a printer for the *New York Daily News*, and my mother was a bookkeeper. They both worked very hard, but fairly or unfairly, I didn't view them as role models for financial success. We lived in the New York City projects. I wanted a financially secure life for myself. I knew it was out there!

I was the first in my family to go to college. I didn't know what I wanted to study; I just knew I wanted to go. My family didn't have the money to send me to an out-of-town school, and so I went to a city school, Brooklyn College, because it was affordable. I majored in education and sociology because I wanted an easy time in college. That's not what I would do today, nor is it what I would advise anyone else to do. My parents could not provide the insight I needed other than to suggest that I become a doctor or a lawyer, but I wasn't interested in either of those professions and did not think I could master the training. I'm not blaming anyone; I'm just stating the facts. They did their best, and all their hard work set an important example for me, but I wanted to escape from Brooklyn.

I had always worked from the time I was old enough to do so. I started ironing shirts for my mother to earn an allowance and understand work. To this day, I enjoy ironing: I find it very calming and satisfying. My first real job was in a post office: I worked as a mail sorter one summer, when I was 15. After that, I worked in retail stores, selling men's clothes. It was easy: I didn't need to have any special training, I liked clothes, and I felt comfortable doing it. My first job in retail was as a salesman in Levine's, a local men's and boys' store, a job I got in high school. It was a successful second-generation family business in a shopping area in Flatbush, near where I lived in Sheepshead Bay.

I knew people who worked at Levine's, and so I walked in one day and asked to see the owner. He hired me because I had the right look to work in a men's clothing store; I was always into fashion, although I didn't realize at the time that I would have a career in it. That wasn't where my head was at.

I'm not suggesting that looks and fashion sense are the key to getting your first job. Some people get hired because they're polite and good-natured, and many business owners want to hire people who will get along well with their coworkers and the customers. Some people get hired because they're very smart and quick to learn. Some people get hired because they're hardworking and that work ethic comes through in the interview. Today my advice to people, young and old, who are looking for a job is to figure out what's special about *you* and find a business that will appreciate that skill or talent or quality. The owner of Levine's was selling children's suits to parents, and so he wanted someone who would present his merchandise well. When I think back on that now, I realize that looks, not substance, got me the job. I had a lot to prove, and I had a lot to learn about life. You need to find what will appeal to the owner or manager of whatever business you want to work in.

I worked at Levine's all through high school, and then I moved on to another retail store in my neighborhood, Bogart's, where I worked part-time throughout my college years. It was in one of the first malls that opened in Brooklyn, the Kings Plaza Shopping Center, and Bogart's was the most prestigious store in that mall: it looked very expensive, with marble floors and beautiful fixtures, and it sold beautiful, expensive clothes. It was a multibrand store that offered the best American brands and emerging designers (such as Polo by Ralph Lauren) as well as European designers. It was like a small Barney's or Bergdorf's.

When I graduated, I didn't have a clue about what to do next. This should relieve some of you who are in school or have graduated recently and are perplexed or panicked about what to do. You're not *supposed* to know. For those of you who have ideas or do know what you want to do—more power to you. The rest of you will reach your destiny by accident: I was a member of that group. I didn't know where to begin my career. All my friends had gone to Europe to celebrate graduation, but I didn't have the money to do that, and I felt responsible for myself and for my future. Therefore, I looked for a job instead: I learned that work ethic from my parents.

Although I enjoyed working at Bogart's, I viewed it as just a job, not the first step toward my future. I had no idea how to start a career. I didn't have a clue how to apply for jobs other than walking in and asking to talk to the manager. I didn't know what was involved in a job interview or how I should prepare for one. I believed I could find success only in Manhattan—which I believed was the big time—not in Brooklyn. I didn't think I would be successful getting paid a commission based on how many suits I sold, and I didn't believe that type of work melded with a college education. Also, I didn't know that retail was a real career, that there were big stores with great training programs that would develop people into future merchants who could rule the industry. I had absolutely no idea how to become successful.

> **Figure out what's special about *you* and find a business that will appreciate that skill or talent or quality.**

I didn't have the right mindset. I didn't go to the finest prep school or graduate from a prestigious university. I didn't intern at Fortune 500 companies. I didn't have any training or preparation to begin a career. I also didn't have any connections or friends whose families had come over on the *Mayflower*. I didn't even know any professionals. I didn't have professors in college who asked me what I was going to do with my life; in fact, my parents didn't even ask me what I planned to do after college: because they didn't have *careers* (they had *jobs*), they thought I would just keep working at Bogart's. I didn't have any mentors or any other role models in my life who could give me advice or direction.

I was prepared to work because I always had, but the only thing I knew how to do was smile, greet people, and sell suits, and being charming would take me only so far. I had a serious desire and drive to make something of myself and to have a better life financially than my parents had. Also, I had traveled a little—nowhere exotic, just to

Florida, the Caribbean, and Central America—with the money I earned at my part-time jobs in college. I loved to travel, and I met interesting people who were different from the people I had grown up with because they were worldlier and had more life experience. Traveling made me realize how sheltered I was and how little I knew of the world. And it triggered a desire in me to have a bigger life. I just needed to figure out how to get started.

I decided I wanted to be a TV newscaster. I was interested in the world around me, it seemed like a cool job, and I liked that newscasters looked and sounded good. I thought I was well-spoken and looked good enough to do that job. Thus, I followed the same tactics I had used in getting jobs in retail. It didn't occur to me that I needed skills and training or that I couldn't just walk in off the street with a heavy New York accent and get a job sitting at a news desk in front of a TV camera.

Yet that was exactly what I tried to do during the summer after I graduated from college. I had a tan, my hair was very long, and I was well dressed (although I had holes in the soles of my shoes, which I covered on the inside with cardboard). I thought I looked terrific! I drove into Manhattan, double-parked in front of the buildings where there were TV stations, and left a friend in the car while I went upstairs to try to get an interview.

The first station I went to was WOR, which was Channel 5 in New York. I walked up to the front desk and said, "I want to interview to be a newscaster. Who do I speak to?" When the receptionist stopped laughing, she said, "You're kidding, right? No one's going to interview you, the way you look." I asked her what she meant, and she said, "You don't look like a newscaster. Where did you go to school? Did you study communications?" When I answered her questions and she realized I knew nothing about the news business, she gave me one piece of advice: "If you're really serious, get a haircut and move to Ohio. I think you have a shot at getting in the front door there."

After a few more encounters like that at other networks, I gave up the idea of becoming a newscaster. I didn't want to cut my hair, and I certainly wasn't going to Ohio to apply for jobs. I needed to find a new idea for what to do with my life; little did I know that inspiration and help can come from the unlikeliest source—if you open yourself up to it.

2

I'll Take Luck Wherever I Can Find It

went back to my job at Bogart's. I didn't know what else to do, so I kept working while I tried to figure it out. Then I got lucky.

One night, I told another salesman that I couldn't get any interviews at what I thought I wanted to do and that I didn't even know how to begin a career. He told me he had a family friend who owned an employment agency and offered to arrange for me to meet him the next day. I was taken aback: I wasn't really asking this guy for help; I was just talking about my situation, yet he had offered to help me find a job. I jumped at the chance.

The next day, I went to the office of Julie Pepper. I told him that I was having trouble finding a job and that no one wanted to interview me because my hair was so long. I asked him for advice, and he said, "I don't think your hair matters; I think what you're about is what matters."

Like most good interviewers, Mr. Pepper instantly sized me up and thought of the fashion industry, which is not as conservative as other workplaces and would appreciate my personal style and fashion sense. He said, "I have something I think would be good for you. It's a great company: Van Heusen." "You mean shirts? Isn't that an old man's company?" I wasn't excited, because to a young guy that company didn't have much appeal: it seemed sleepy to me. He said, "It's not just shirts. It's a very good, solid company, and I think it's the perfect place for you to start." Mr. Pepper asked me to trust him. I did—mostly because I was desperate to get a real job—and I found out soon enough that Van Heusen was a public company and one of the top three shirt manufacturers in the United States. I don't know if Jules Pepper specialized in recruiting for the fashion industry or if he had jobs in other industries in mind, but this was what he offered me. He also sold me on the company when he said it was looking for smart young people with fashion sense and he thought I would like working there.

Since that day, I've met many people who had a similar experience but didn't listen to the person trying to help them. They thought they knew more than the person making the suggestion, or they didn't like the company or the industry or the job being offered, and so they just ignored the advice. I don't know what would have happened to me if I hadn't accepted my coworker's offer to meet with Jules Pepper or if I hadn't agreed to go on the interview that Mr. Pepper recommended. All I know is that interview led me to a company I worked at for 33 years as I climbed the ladder from the bottom all the way to the top, and I owe both of them so much for that.

Mr. Pepper was my first mentor, and I learned that you never can tell where or how a mentor may appear. Ever since, I've kept my eyes and ears—and my mind—open to new opportunities and new possibilities, and that mindset has never failed me. I firmly believe you should always answer when opportunity knocks, because you never know what or who is going to be on the other side of that door. I could just as easily have said "No, thanks" to the salesman at work, thinking, I don't want to meet with an *employment agency*; I want an interview with *an actual company* that can hire me. Or I might have thought that it would be a waste of my time, that meeting this guy wouldn't lead to anything. I believe, however, that you should always accept someone's offer to help and make new contacts because you never know where they may lead. In my case, that meeting led eventually to my becoming the CEO of a $2 billion company. Jules Pepper also prepped me on how to answer the questions he thought I would be asked at the interview. Today, of course, everyone knows (or should know) that when you interview for a job, you have to be really prepared. You need to know something about the company that's interviewing you, and it's especially important to consider what's important to that company and why you might fit the bill.

The first question Mr. Pepper asked me was, "What do you want to do?" I said, "I don't have a clue." That obviously wasn't the right answer, but since I *didn't* know what I wanted to do, I didn't know how to answer this question. I tried again: "I'd like to work in a big company in New York." Mr. Pepper said that wasn't the right answer either. He told me I should say that I'm *fascinated* by the fashion business, that I've *always* wanted to work in the apparel industry, and that I really want to work hard and learn as much as I can about the business. I thought, Okay, I can do that.

Then he asked me, "How much do you want to make?" and I said, "As much as I can." He said, "That's not the answer. Let's try again: How much do you want to earn?" I pulled a number out of the sky and said $25,000. He said, "That's not the answer. The answer is, 'It doesn't matter.' Of course, everybody needs money to live, but when you're starting your career, that's the last thing you should think about. Instead, you need to consider more important factors: Is this a good company? Is it in an industry you'll like working in? Will they train you? Does this company promote from within? Do you have a chance to succeed? Do they treat people well?" I had never heard anyone talk in those terms, and what he said made a lot of sense to me.

His advice paid off. The very next day I had an interview at Phillips-Van Heusen (now PVH). The company was founded by the Phillips family in Pottsville, Pennsylvania, in the early 1900s. Originally, it manufactured shirts and sold them to coal miners as they exited the mine, but over the years the company had expanded its product line and locations well beyond that. It owned retail stores, a sweater mill, and a suit company, though shirts were still the cash cow of the business, bringing in $250 million a year at that time.

The office was at 417 Fifth Avenue, four blocks north of the Empire State Building in midtown Manhattan. I was supposed to meet with Sid Goldman, the vice president and general merchandise manager, but when I arrived, his assistant came out and said, "Mr. Goldman isn't ready yet; would you mind waiting in Alan's office?"

Alan was a very good-looking guy in his mid-twenties, an impeccable dresser, very sophisticated, with a great sense of style, which impressed me. I still had some misgivings about working for "an old man's shirt company," but when I met Alan and saw there were other young people working there, I started to feel like this company might be a good fit for me after all.

Alan was busy: he was packing up some things, as though he was going on a trip, yet he was willing to talk as he did so. I was only mildly interested in the conversation until I asked him where he was going, and he said he was going to Europe. I immediately thought of all my friends who were backpacking through Europe while I was looking for a job, and I asked him where he was going on his vacation. Alan said, "I'm not going on vacation; I'm going on business to Paris, Milan, London, all the fashion capitals. I'm a designer, so I travel several times a year to Europe and other places to find ideas and inspiration that I apply to what we do here."

When he said that, I was sold. I made up my mind right then and there that if I could get to Europe on business by working for this company, I really wanted the job. Plus, I would be working in Manhattan.

Now I wanted to know even more. Since the job I was interviewing for was as an assistant designer, I asked Alan how long it had taken him to get from assistant to designer. He said, "About a year and a half." I thought to myself, I don't know how good this guy is, but I know I can do what he does. I was very competitive, and so I was already thinking that I would have to beat his record to get promoted. But first I had to get the job.

At that moment, though I didn't really know it consciously, I was establishing my first goals in business. To succeed in business, you must know what needs to be done and how to get there. My first goal was simple: get the job! And then become a designer in less time than Alan.

By the way, Alan turned out to be Alan Flusser, one of the first gurus of men's fashion. He went on to have his own house of design and write a number of the best menswear style guides that were ever written (I have them all in my home library). As I said before, you never know who is going to be on the other side of the door when opportunity knocks.

Fast-forward a half hour later, when I was called into the interview with Mr. Goldman. Since I now knew I wanted the job, it didn't matter to me anymore what Van Heusen was or wasn't. I was interested, and I was impressed. Now I just had to impress my interviewer.

Fortunately, I was dressed really well in a three-piece suit with a European cut. I had learned a lot about men's fashion from selling high-end suits to our clientele, and one of the perks of working at a men's store was that I could buy clothes for 50 percent off. The salesmen had to look good, and so we needed to wear high-quality clothes. And thanks to Jules Pepper, I had an idea of what this company was looking for and how I might be able to impress my interviewer.

Sure enough, the first question Mr. Goldman asked was, "What is it you want to accomplish?" With Mr. Pepper's coaching in my head,

I answered, "I'm fascinated by the fashion business and have always wanted to work in this industry. I want to learn. I want to be with a good company that is proud of its products and is willing to train someone like me who will work hard and smart to do whatever is needed." Then he asked me, "Do you have an idea what you want to earn?" I replied, "Money is not an issue with me; it doesn't matter. What matters is learning. I want to learn and contribute. I'm sure the money will take care of itself."

Every question Mr. Goldman asked me was one that Mr. Pepper had given me the right answer to. I've often said, "I know what I know, and I know what I don't know." I was always grounded, and to this day I don't care where the next good idea comes from. Jules Pepper talked to me for only about 30 minutes, but in that short time he taught me valuable lessons: Be precise and focus only on the important issue or issues. The first job should be all about learning. Have a goal: get the job!

Mr. Goldman hired me that day as an assistant designer (I was essentially a clerk). I was so excited that I immediately called my mother: "You're never going to believe this! I got the job—with a salary of $8,500 a year. And not only that, I'm on the executive payroll!" I didn't know what that meant; I only knew it sounded good. It wasn't until later that I discovered it meant I was exempt from overtime pay for the zillions of hours I would work, so I was the lowest-paid guy in the company. (Of course, over time I got even, but that's getting ahead of the story.)

It didn't matter what they were paying me: I was on my way. That entry-level job led to more and greater responsibilities over the course of 33 years. I started at the bottom and worked my way up all the way to the top. I've often heard the expression "The harder I work, the luckier I get." I don't know who said it, but it absolutely applies to my life and career. As a result, I have a few lessons of my own I'd like to pass on to you.

> The first job should be all about learning. Have a goal: get the job!

When you're interviewing for a job, you need to work hard to understand who you're going to be meeting with and what might be important to that person. If you're interviewing for a job with a particular fashion or luxury brand, there are many places you can research that brand and get a sense of what's important to it, and I don't mean just doing research on the Internet.

Yes, it's important to go online, look at the company's website, and read everything you can about the company you're interviewing with, including all the articles written about it. Know who the CEO is and who some of the top people at the company are and see if you can find anything written about them too. Google your interviewer (if you know in advance who you'll be meeting with) and see if there are any articles about him or her. Find out what the CEO and the president and other key people talk about when they're interviewed by the media and learn what they find important so that you can discuss that if you have the opportunity during your interview. Look at the company's advertising to get a sense of how it presents itself and what it is trying to convey to its customers.

However, if you're interviewing for a brand that has retail stores or is sold through department stores or chain stores, you also need to visit as many of those stores as you can before the interview. Ask the people working there, How's business? How's traffic? When do you get new deliveries? When do you put merchandise on sale? What are your best items? If something is out of stock in my size, can you get it for me? Do you ship overseas?

Then come up with your own point of view about what works and doesn't work in the store, what impresses you and what puts you off. Look at the way the people who work there are dressed and think about whether their clothing and fashion sense and style represents the brands they're selling—or doesn't. Many luxury brands have their employees wear uniforms: Do you know why? In the world of fashion, it's easy to do this type of research, so don't ignore it and think you can talk your way to getting a job simply by reading about the designer, wholesaler, or retailer you're interviewing with.

For some jobs, it's more difficult to do this type of research, but in many industries, especially anything in consumer products—automobiles, books, computers, electronics, food, furniture, and office supplies, to name just a few—it's easy to get a sense of a company's products. If you're interested in working at Colgate-Palmolive, look at Colgate toothpaste and the many other products it makes. Look at the packaging: see how the company presents itself and its product. Look at what the point of differentiation is: How is Colgate different from other toothpastes on the market? This is what you need to know so that you're prepared for an interview.

In my case, I had the benefit of talking to someone who knew the company I was going to interview with. Jules Pepper advised me what was important to the company and what they would be looking for, and having that information in advance helped me get the job. Some people might say I just got lucky by meeting Mr. Pepper, but as the chapter title says, I'll take luck wherever I can find it. That good fortune merely got me an interview. I still needed to prove myself and get the job: I had to be convincing. They had to see the excitement in my eyes, the interest and the energy I would bring to my work. And once I got the job, I had to work hard to do well.

3

What a Difference a Day Makes

The following Monday was my first day of work at PVH, and I was introduced to my new boss, Bruce Klatsky. He impressed me right away because he seemed so much older than I was: he was so self-confident and poised. Actually, he was only six months older than I, but I found out later that he came from a somewhat wealthy family and his father was a successful businessman. Bruce had gone to the right schools, and he wasn't like the guys I had grown up with in Brooklyn, who talked like they were just trying to be cool. Bruce was a businessman, and he was ambitious.

The first thing he did was look me up and down, and then he said, "You're my new assistant? Okay, you'll do."

Then he explained: "I guess I'm not important enough for me to hire my own assistant, but I figure we can work this out. Let me tell you something about me. I intend to be president of this company someday, and if you want to come with me, you're going to have to do what I need you to do. I not only need to understand this business as well as anybody—and better—but I also need you to come in early or stay very late or both, because that's when you're going to do your job. The rest of the time I need you to go wherever I go so you can learn how to do *my* job. I need to teach you everything I know, because I want to be promoted as quickly as I can, and the only way I can do that is if you're ready to replace me."

I couldn't believe what I was hearing. Some people might have been daunted by Bruce telling them they would have to do two jobs, but I wasn't daunted at all; I was impressed and excited. I saw that my new boss had a clear vision of where he wanted to go and understood how important the people who worked for him were to help him get there. I saw he was someone I could learn from, a person who had his head in the right place. He wasn't threatened by the people working for him, worrying that they were after his job; instead, he *wanted* me to take over his job so that he could move even higher in the company. The minute I met Bruce, I knew I wanted to work for him, and I hoped I would follow him all the way to the top of the company.

There are many times in a person's career when you meet your boss and know right away whether this is someone you should follow to the ends of the earth or someone you should get away from as quickly as you can. Bruce was someone to follow. And sure enough, he eventually became president of the corporation, and he and I worked together for the next 33 years. He went straight up the ladder, and I also made it to the top, though with a lot of zigzags along the way.

You need to recognize luck when it comes your way. I had always been grounded. I didn't take risks with my future. I didn't give in to peer pressure and do things I didn't want to do. I was never wild; I was always careful and measured in the way I conducted myself, from my very first jobs. I wanted to see if I had a shot at being successful, because at an early age I saw people who were successful. When I started out in business, I was very focused on doing the right thing. I didn't care what I had to do to succeed: I would do anything anyone asked me to do. I would have swept the floors.

I also recognized—and accepted—what was being offered to me. I wanted to learn, and I was being given that opportunity. When you start a job in a new company and meet the people you're going to be working with and for, it's important to draw conclusions about them. You need to figure out—quickly—if they can do what they're supposed to do to make the company successful, if they're people you can learn from, whether they're closed-minded or open-minded, and whether you're investing your time and your career and your potential success with the right people.

If you think, Yes, these are people I can learn from and can succeed with, you're in a great position at your new job. But if you think they're not, you have to recognize that this job is just a foot in the door and that you'll learn what you can while you work here. You also need to plan your next move to a better place with better people who will help you succeed in your career just as you help that company succeed. Work is a two-way street: if you're working hard to help a company succeed, you should be rewarded not merely by being paid but also by learning how to do even more. If you want to be successful, don't waste your valuable time and energy working hard in a company that's not going to help you get ahead and succeed in your career.

Whether it's your first job, your second job, or any job you take at any time in your life, *you* are responsible for reading the people you're going to be working for and with. Maybe you can't tell immediately, but you'll know within a week or a month whether your boss and your coworkers have the character and the expertise to teach you. If they're great, you've got a great star to follow, so make sure you impress those people and work as hard as you need to to get to where you want to be.

There's also a chance you're going to work for the wrong people. I wasn't always lucky enough to work for someone like Bruce, because I didn't always report directly to him. At one point I worked for a guy who was one of the most miserable human beings in the world and an absolute SOB to work for. I went to work every day knowing the company appreciated what I was doing, but I was very unhappy that I had to put up with this guy. Nevertheless, I knew I had to stay the course and work as hard as I could in the hopes of getting out from under him.

Fortunately, the system works. One day, I was at a sales convention when one of the vice presidents asked me how I was doing. I said I was doing great: I always tried to be upbeat and cheerful no matter what I was really feeling about my job or my work. He said, "I'm glad to hear you say that, but I know you're not doing great. Everyone in senior management knows you're working for one of the meanest SOBs in the world—who's still at the company because we think he can do a good job for us right now—but your goal in your career here should be to survive this guy. You'll outlast him: we're confident of that."

I was glad to hear it, and that was another lesson I learned: even when you're working for a miserable boss, you have to get yourself noticed by others in the company and let them respect you for who you are. If you do that, it doesn't matter in the end who you're working for. You'll have a future in the company if you do your job right.

And I did survive him: after about a year, I was given a different job working for someone else. And eventually that miserable guy committed career suicide. He was so unpleasant and angered so many suppliers and customers that we started to lose business. The company realized he needed to go. Good riddance!

That's often what happens: the system works. People get to where they get to because they *deserve* to be there. Staying there is another story, but there are no flukes in business: if you're good and you handle yourself well, you'll get there. The opposite is also true: if you do something wrong in business and you don't tell anybody, it comes back to haunt you. It might be a week or a month or a year later, but what you did never goes away. You can't shovel anything under the rug.

Finally, if you realize you're working for the wrong people, *you* have to decide about your future. Can you distinguish yourself in the company while working for this individual? If not, what are you going to do about it? You have only a few choices. You can dig in and say, I don't care what this person is like; I'm going to do what I need to do to be recognized and appreciated, and my work will prove itself. Or you need to decide that at the appropriate time you're either going to ask for a transfer or leave the company. But in the meantime you have to be prepared to work for difficult people as well as great ones.

> Even when you're working for a miserable boss, you have to get yourself noticed by others in the company and let them respect you for who you are.

In my case, eventually I got a new boss. Also, my company saw I not only was doing a good job but was able to deal with difficult situations and difficult people, which is an important skill to have. Not everybody is sweet, and business is not necessarily fair. You just need to decide how you're going to deal with the difficulties and the miserable people you encounter during your career. You are responsible for your own success; nobody else is.

4

Youth Is Wasted on the Young

During my first few months at PVH, I was often concerned about my lack of experience. I was not only the new guy, I was also the youngest person working there, and I was always the junior executive in the room. However, in spite of my entry-level position, my company wanted me to learn, and so I was always included in the mix.

One day I was invited to have lunch with many senior people from the company who were meeting with the president of a multi-billion-dollar textile company. I was happy simply to be invited. When we got to the restaurant, the textile company president asked me to sit next to him at the table, and I'll never forget what he said: "Mark, do you know why I'm sitting next to you? Because *you are the future.*"

I was a bit surprised, but I was also impressed, and I thanked him. I realized this guy was special because he had a long-term perspective on his company, my company, and our industry in general. He taught me a lesson I remember to this day: even though you're the youngest, newest, or least experienced person in the room, you may be the most important person because you are someone who will be making the important decisions someday and because you are plugged in to what's going on far more than is anyone older than you. Young people need to understand and respect that and realize that they have something to contribute. (Of course, the way you present yourself is also very important, and I'll talk about that in Chapter 14.)

Moreover, because the president of this company introduced himself and took an interest in me, I had a direct connection to him, which I was able to leverage as I worked my way up in my company. I was able to call him directly, ask him for advice, and show him ideas I was working on to get his input. That connection was invaluable because I could learn from him just as he was learning from me.

Most young people don't realize their youth is something senior executives covet. Although there are some very confident, self-possessed exceptions, most people just starting out worry that they don't have any experience or training even if they are very well educated. They're intimidated by the people they're working with, who seem fearless: they know what they're doing, they've done it before, and they seem to know how to handle every difficult situation and problem that arises.

But don't sell yourself short. The fact that you're young or new to your company is not a negative; it's a positive, and you should always keep that in mind even as you're learning. You know more than you think you do. Young people are closer to what's new: they're simply wired in better. As a result, most companies—if they have smart managers running them—covet the opinions of young people. No matter how much TV I watch or new music I listen to, no matter how involved I am with Facebook, Instagram, Twitter, Pinterest, or the next new thing, I realize now that I'll never be fully tapped in to what younger people know about our constantly changing culture and technologies.

The fact that you're young or new to your company is not a negative; it's a positive.

I have this opinion because of the way I rose through the ranks of my company. I didn't grow up on the financial side (although I certainly understand the financials of a business), and so I view business from a different angle, and my approach works. It's good to have a different way of looking at things, and young people from different backgrounds and with different experiences have something to contribute. You have to know when to talk and when not to talk. You need to know what questions to ask and what not to ask. Nonetheless, every one of your thoughts and questions has value. Don't let anyone sell you short and don't waste your youth, because you're only young once.

5

The Godfather

I started in the design process in product development and discovered there were meetings at which all the designers presented their ideas for the next product range and the senior merchants edited them. In effect, they decided what would be produced—and what wouldn't be.

These meetings were often hugely disappointing: after all, we product designers worked hard to put together a collection, and then the senior people would say, "Yes, no, yes, no, yes, no." The good managers would usually explain why they decided yea or nay, which enabled us to learn from these meetings, but some managers just gave a thumbs-up or thumbs-down, as though they were at the Roman Colosseum. I found that very frustrating, but it was just the way they did things, and we had to accept it when they didn't explain. Clearly, someone else was editing my work and someone else was making the decisions.

I realized that if I didn't understand the totality of the business, if I couldn't see the global perspective, I would never be in charge of my ideas. I would be edited for the rest of my career, and that started to bother me. That was why learning more about merchandising—especially in terms of inventory management—became important to me. That was why sales became important to me. It became my passion to learn other disciplines even though developing product was my forte. Learning drove everything I did, mostly things that were not creative. I realized that the more information I had, the greater control I would have over the decision-making process. I did get that broad-based knowledge; I'll talk about that later, in Chapter 12.

Ever since I saw the movie *The Godfather*, I have been impressed by the logo, an image of a hand holding two perpendicular wooden bars that maneuver the strings to a marionette. I realized it was relevant to my career—and it's relevant to your career, too. In the fashion business, many people study design because they love the creative process, they want to be designers, and they assume they will be in control of what they design. There's only one way to get there aside from being talented. The only way they can be in control of their designs is to understand all the other disciplines as well. For people who work in marketing, for example, if all they know is how to create exciting advertising and they don't understand how it sells product or how it affects the price of a product or other technical factors, they're never going to be in control.

When I saw this symbol of *The Godfather*, I realized it applied to me and my career: when I started working, it quickly became clear that I could be at the *end* of those strings, with somebody controlling me and telling me what to do, or I could be *holding* those strings because I knew how everything worked together.

That's the moral of this story. It doesn't matter what you love in a business or where your passion lies; you can't know only that one thing. Instead, you have to learn all the disciplines. You have to be interested in things that don't interest you. That doesn't mean you have to be proficient in them, but you have to respect them and learn them. If you do that, you can grow and succeed and climb the ladder and become the puppet master instead of just a puppet.

However, the flip side is true, too: if you don't want to invest the time and energy in learning about the finances of your business, and the inventory management, and the production process, and the marketing and advertising and selling, you'll have to be content with succeeding in just the one area of your business that you know really well. That's okay if that's all you want, but you'll never be in control of your ideas.

Decide what you really want to be in your career. Puppet or puppet master?

6

Ask Not What Your Company Can Do for You

While you're climbing the ladder to your own success, it's important to remember that you also strive to make your company more successful. That's really what you were hired to do, so that goal should be ever present in your mind.

After I had been working at Phillips-Van Heusen for about nine months, I was an assistant designer. Although I worked in New York, part of my job was to visit the factories where PVH actually made the shirts we sold. At the time, we had 10 factories and were headquartered in Pottsville, Pennsylvania, a small town about 100 miles northwest of Philadelphia, in the heart of coal country. I had just joined the group, and so I was very interested in learning as much as possible about the factory and manufacturing and the work relationship between the designers and the manufacturers.

In my first month in this new position, I visited the Pottsville factory at least four times, and by the end of the second month I had gotten to know the people who worked there. I went with a team the first few times and watched the interactions between the factory people and the designers and product development people. The factory people were mainstream Americans, and many were operationally oriented engineers who wore short-sleeve shirts with pocket protectors. In stark contrast, the New York people were urban and dressed in trendy suits, and they were more focused on marketing and design, with an eye toward fashion and style. These were two very different cultures, and the more I watched and listened to them interact, the more I saw that the two groups didn't mix properly. Even worse, they weren't working *together* very well because of the difference in their backgrounds and responsibilities.

This was especially interesting to me because I knew that manufacturing costs were one of our biggest issues. Offshore production was just starting to become a serious threat, and every U.S. manufacturing company was trying to find a way to compete with imports that were manufactured at much lower cost than the same American products. There are several ways a company can compete: faster time to market, higher-quality products, and more flexible operations that can produce new designs and new products quickly. However, more often than not, most commodity products compete primarily on price. Therefore, the lower your costs are, the more profit you can make. That's just Business 101.

As I watched the New York design people meet with the Pennsylvania factory people, I noticed the dilemma presented by the two cultures working against each other rather than with each other. The factory people were trying to reduce costs through mass production, because if they had to buy special dyes or special tooling, or stop and start production to change a button style or thread color, that reduced efficiency and cost more money. However, if they could use the same buttons, threads, labels, and shape of pockets over and over, their manufacturing process could become very efficient and cost-competitive. That would also enable the company to keep a proportion of production in the United States, where it could still be hands-on, rather than moving to China, for instance.

Meanwhile, the New York fashion people were focused on creating *new* designs, not *consistent* designs. For example, the designers believed that changing the pocket shape by a quarter of an inch was more important than mass production even if that would save a quarter per pocket. Twenty-five cents might not seem like much money, but when you multiply it by the millions of shirts we were making, you're suddenly costing the company hundreds of thousands of dollars.

The first few times I sat in on these discussions, I simply watched and listened. After a few weeks of hearing the same thing, however, I said to myself, This isn't working. Both sides were trying to present their viewpoint politely, but I could see this was a culture clash: the factory people thought that cost was more important, and the New Yorkers thought that design was more important. Also, the New York people simply did not want to budge and give up creative control. Moreover,

I knew the New Yorkers were wrong even though I was one of them. I was dictated to by design and respected product above all else. But men don't pick their dress shirts for the shape of the pocket—and a quarter of an inch difference? Nonsense! There were more significant ways we could differentiate our products, such as collar, fit, color, pattern, and package.

The next time I visited the Pottsville factory, I happened to go alone, without my two supervisors, and so I decided to talk to the head of product development. I said, "If you give me a list of all the factors that are critical to helping you reduce costs, I will do my best to go back to the management in New York and try to make changes. But I need specific information and what the savings will be." Sure enough, he said he would give me a list, which he did later that day. The opportunity for savings without reducing quality was extraordinary. I returned to the New York office and shared this list with my boss. Unknown to me, when I left, the head of product development went in to see the senior vice president and head of manufacturing.

About a week later, the chairman of the board, Larry Phillips, asked to see me. I was surprised, because this was the first time I was called into his office. He said he had heard I was spending a lot of time in Pottsville, and I said, "I'm trying to learn as much as I can. I'm trying to make sure we do everything we can to stay competitive and keep costs down without sacrificing the quality of our products." Then he said, "I want to tell you a story. My grandfather started this company in 1881. My father has been with the company for 50 years, I've been working here for 30 years, and our head of manufacturing has been running the Pottsville factory for 40 years. He just called to tell me that you are *the first person* from New York to sit down with real earnestness and ask what the manufacturing people really need to be successful! Mark, I don't know how this is going to turn out, but when you do something like that, it gets noticed, even though you might not think so."

I scored big points with our chairman that day (and with the factory people) simply because I kept an open mind. I'm not telling this story to show how smart I was on this occasion. (Actually, my humble beginnings allowed me to relate humbly to the manufacturing group. I was comfortable with them in spite of my New York lifestyle.) My purpose is to show you that it's important to have an open mind with people from all walks of life and all cultures even if the differences are simply those between Pennsylvanians and New Yorkers.

It's critical to truly *listen* to what's important to people in other departments and functions in your company. Most of the time, they know what they're doing, they have experience and skills that you don't have, and they have the best interests of the company at heart. Sure, you're going to find people in every business who don't want to work as hard as you do (or as you want *them* to) or who put their personal agenda before the goals of the company as a whole. You'll even find some people who like to thwart others because of internal politics. But most of your colleagues are trying to do their jobs in the best way they know how. Therefore, you should check your ego at the door, get past your culture differences, find out what's really important to the success of your company as a whole, and try to effect change.

I had absolutely no personal agenda when it came to my job. I had only one interest: What's best for the company? If it helped the company, it would help me. I had no motive other than doing the right thing, which was to have the most cost-effective product. That was the most important thing to our company at that time.

For other companies, the opposite is true. For example, there are many luxury brands that would rather manufacture their products in Hong Kong to reduce costs and increase profits. However, "Made in France" and "Made in Italy" is more important than price for those luxury products. Doing what's best for your company applies in both situations: you need to understand what the crucial elements are for success at *your* company. Sometimes that means you need to cut through the clutter, make sure you have no ego, and look at what's important to your company as a whole.

In this case, my helping the company cut costs and enabled us to produce more competitively and forestall the decision to close the plant. When you do the right thing for your company, it often pays off for you. In my case, I was promoted to designer later that week, in less time than it had taken Alan Flusser.

7

Climbing
the Ladder

I was so excited when I got my first promotion: I recognized that move as only the first step up the ladder. I was very, very determined to keep moving up and do everything I could to make a success of myself. Part of my work ethic was to be seen as someone who would do anything, to show people that no task was beneath me.

When you get your foot in a company's door, you have to show your boss and the people around you that you're the go-to person, that no task is too big or too small. They need to know that whatever area or job you're involved in, no matter how big the challenge is, you will be willing to tackle it and get it done. Even if you don't know how to do the particular assignment or task or responsibility that's handed to you, you have to be seen as someone who is smart enough to figure out who to talk to and find someone who can help you. It's extremely important to be seen as one of those people management can rely on to get the job done. Go out of your way to meet people and ask all of them what they do. Ask if you can you sit in on meetings. Ask people if there is something you can help with if you have some time.

I asked questions that others maybe never asked or thought to ask, and when I was working my way up, I could see in the eyes of the people I talked to that they had confidence in me, that they felt comfortable asking me to do things they might not have asked someone else to do, for example, to work late or on weekends. If people like you and see that you're a go-to problem solver, chances are that you're going to get more exposure and be given more opportunities.

This ties in to the issue of whether you should stay with one company or leave and explore other opportunities at other companies. When I was starting out in my career, it was a badge of honor to spend a long period at one company and move up the ladder. That was respected because it showed that apparently you were doing something right: if the company continued to advance you and give you new opportunities and you excelled at them, you would move up the ladder. In the current business world, the model is very different, because companies look for people with multiple and varied work experience.

For example, someone starting out today might work for a time at a company such as J.Crew, which has a reputation for really understanding how to develop product. Then you might work for a company such as Ralph Lauren, which has a great understanding of men's fashion, and then for a company such as Donna Karan, which has a great reputation for women's fashion. Then, if you're lucky enough, you might work for a company such as Louis Vuitton, which has an extraordinary reputation for luxury goods. If you moved up each time you changed jobs, you might consider that career path to be more exciting than staying at one company for your entire career or a good part of it. Either path can work: climbing the ladder at only one company or rotating through different companies.

I believe you're more important to the company than the company is to you. You might not feel that way when you're working and thinking, Am I doing the right thing by staying here? Am I going to get the next raise? Am I going to be promoted? Do I have a future at this company, or should I move on? But companies need qualified people, and when they find people they feel are really good, they want to do everything they can within their power to keep those people. Somewhere along the way in your career, you need to understand that leverage you have.

If you're getting multiple assignments and promotions consistently within a one- or two-year period and if you are learning more in different areas of responsibility, I'd advise you to ignore the current thinking and run the course to see how far you can get in your current company. If this is not the case and your career is stagnant, you have to consider that it may be time to leave. Also, moving from one company to the next can be profitable, because when you're homegrown in a company, you're being compensated fairly but you won't be as richly rewarded as you will be when you move to higher-level positions at different companies.

In my case, I had 25 different assignments at PVH in my first 25 years, culminating in president of the company (I moved up from there, too). I started as a creative person in the boys' division (which they had at the time). That was a great place for me to start because it was a smaller division in the company and the profits weren't as robust as those in other divisions, so the company didn't have as extensive a staff there; that meant I could do more and experience a wider area of responsibilities, and I could move up more easily. In the rest of the company and in many other companies, there are departments devoted to specific apparel—a shirt department, a sportswear department, a children's department, and so forth—and in each of those departments there are specialists. There's a designer for dress shirts, another for sports shirts, another for sweaters, and another for pants. What happens in those departments is that the staffing structure devolves into "stovepipes": in other words, employees get pigeonholed in one department, and the only way to advance is to move straight up the stovepipe. That structure doesn't allow you to move around and learn different disciplines, and that can limit your career.

When I started as an assistant designer, I was designing boys' dress shirts. My boss was the VP of the children's department, and she was a knitwear expert, and so she taught me knitwear. Within a year and a half, I replaced her. I was then responsible for learning sweaters, knitwear, pants, and many other categories. Thus, I had a head start on everyone else because I was already moving up in the company. Learning entirely new disciplines is a great reason to stay with one company.

Very often in business today, it's almost as if you're given an index card with your name on it that says you're a salesperson, and so for the rest of your career you're a salesperson. You're not trained cross-channel, and so it's very hard to leave that stovepipe to get into merchandising or design. You have to be very lucky, your company has to like you, and you have to be determined to put aside your expertise in one area (or use it as a lever) to go into something totally new and really excel at it.

I was very fortunate that I had a head start because I had multicategory experience under me, whereas everyone I was competing with was a specialist. That was one of the reasons I moved up so rapidly in terms of salary and expertise: I had more to offer. I put myself in a position to learn everything I could about everything I could. You need to do the same thing if you want to move up in your company: keep your eyes open, recognize that knowing only one discipline could be a deterrent, and realize that if you are really striving to get ahead, you need to understand more than one area of your business.

I realize that some companies may not encourage or even allow their employees to move around the way I'm advocating. Some managers may feel that they hired you to do a specific job, and if you're excelling at it—*especially* if you're excelling at it—they don't want you to leave that job to move to another department. They may feel they need you doing exactly what you're doing. To avoid that situation, you need to make sure to talk to the right people (while still doing a great job) and put it in their heads that you have an interest in something else and would like to pursue it.

This approach works only if you're well liked. Moreover, you need to show that you want to be loyal to and stay with the company but also have a need to learn. You need to present your case extremely convincingly: for example, say something like "I understand that I'm important in this division, and I will continue to do my job here well, but at the same time, could I start learning after work, or sit in on meetings in other areas, or take on some small assignments from someone working in another discipline?" If your company likes you, it will be willing to do something extra for you.

Asking to be included is usually considered a great thing. It shows that you're interested in learning more, you care about the product, and you want to move forward in your career. You might run into politics, because there may be three other people like you who also are doing a similar job and want to learn. To stand out in that situation, you need to present yourself well, make a compelling case for why you should be included, and work yourself into the political structure of your company. Make a friend. Impress people. Ask if you can help them.

In my case, I was still working in the small division of boyswear, but the men's shirt division was where all the money was made, and my work started to get noticed because everything I did was in really good taste. The company instructed the men's shirt designers to come look at my work to see what I was doing. That sent a signal to management that maybe they should have me work in a more important capacity or area of the business. And they did.

First, they moved me from the kids' division to the sportswear division; then they moved me to the cash cow, the men's shirt division. They gave me the title of fashion director, which was really a merchant's job overseeing all the design work. From there, the company developed sportswear collections—outerwear, pants, shirts, and sweaters—with everything under one roof, and I was earmarked to be one of the lead merchants to head up a division to put the collection business together within the company. That's a lot of different assignments, and that's how I was able to learn so much about so many areas of the business. Then my first real leap to another discipline was merchandising, where I started to learn the numbers. But I'm getting ahead of the story again.

Smart companies lose their people to themselves.

Even when I was still working as a children's designer, it wasn't enough for me to know that there was a printed T-shirt business in which, for example, we could take a picture of a tiger and put it on the chest of a shirt. For me, it wasn't enough to know this could be done; I wanted to understand the manufacturing process. I wanted to know, How does the picture stick to the shirt? Where do these materials come from? How long does it take to make one, and how many can you make in an hour? I had this incredible thirst for knowledge. As I started to learn more, that was when it became clear to me that designing was not my forte, but I could be the one holding the strings of that marionette I wrote about in Chapter 5. You need to decide what you want to do with your career and then make it happen. But most important, remember that "smart companies lose their people to themselves."

8

Once in My Life
I Was Brilliant

When I had been with the company for about three years, I was given an opportunity to join the largest division of the corporation in a product development role. I was only 26 years old at the time, and I wasn't really ready for the job. In fact, I probably wasn't ready for most of the promotions I was given in my early years. However, I had confidence, I had faith in my ability, and I had training. I was driven! When I was given this big job, I knew I had to grow into it, but I also knew I would somehow be able to figure things out and solve problems as they arose. I didn't plan on disrupting the system during my first month.

As was mentioned in Chapter 7, my new position was fashion director for men's dress shirts, but the job also encompassed the business management side of product development. I had three creative people reporting to me who were responsible for building our shirt collection. There was an established two-part process for doing this.

The first part involved several large textile mills in the United States, which we visited to see their view of the future for our products in terms of which textile designs were going to be trending in the future season. Then our people would select and purchase from their textile offerings and craft a shirt collection. The problem with this part of the process was that the textile mills were showing their textile collections to everyone in the United States, and so there was nothing exclusive about what they were showing us. If they showed me a particular stripe or a particular color and I picked it for my product line, another shirt company could just as easily pick the same stripe or color for its product line. That's not a desirable situation: obviously, we didn't want our new products looking like everyone else's. Yet this was accepted as the norm.

The second part of the textile-sourcing process was done through *converters,* who were essentially middlemen. These were entrepreneurs of U.S.-based businesses who traveled to Japan, Indonesia, Malaysia, Taiwan, Korea, and elsewhere to have textiles designed for manufacturing into garments that would be produced in the United States. By buying textiles internationally, U.S. companies could obtain fabric of a finer quality at a lower price because the imports came from countries where the overhead was less expensive than it was in the United States. The minimum quantities in these countries were manageable, and so they would support exclusivity.

The first time I visited these converters, I was surprised by how simple their presentations were. For example, they showed me a black-striped shirt they had bought in Italy. Then they painted a picture of a burgundy shirt and a picture of a hunter green shirt as alternative colors to illustrate that this particular shirt was offered in three colors. These samples represented their ideas for their textile collection, and they used them to quote us a price. These collections were more exclusive than the collections we were offered at the U.S. textile mills, and we would purchase the fabrics.

For the first month in my new job, I watched this process: I saw the team buy some fabric from the U.S. textile mills and then buy some exclusive fabric designs from the international converters (the middlemen) and put together a collection of shirts for the next season. As I watched, I thought, What makes these people think they know more about the future of shirts than we do? After all, we were the third largest shirt company in the world. Even if we were the smallest shirt company in the world, we would still know more about shirt designs than the textile converters did because we sold directly to the retail channel and ultimately to consumers. Why were we allowing them to go to Europe (or any other port of call) and purchase ideas that they then painted and showed to us, with a price quote that seemed completely arbitrary? I had no idea where their prices were coming from, and the entire process bothered me.

Meanwhile, the fabrics that we bought from international sources (via the converters) were shipped from Taiwan, Japan, or Korea (and other countries) to our warehouses in Pottsville and Schuylkill Haven, Pennsylvania. As it turned out, one of my responsibilities was to identify these designs (imported fabrics) and match them to the cutting tickets, or the production plan. Often labeling was confused or designs and styles changed, yet nothing could slow down the manufacturing plants. I needed to travel back and forth from the New York office to our Pennsylvania factories, identify each fabric, and match it with the product we wanted to make. Because I was closely associated with the factory group, I was well accepted and had easy access. I noticed that each fabric had the name of the textile mill it came from printed on the edge (called the *selvage*)—not the name of the converter's company but the actual name of the mill that manufactured the products. The converters never revealed what textile companies they bought from, but the names were printed on the fabric itself!

Because all my previous positions had been on the creative side, I didn't know much about the operations side of the business; nevertheless, this process didn't make any sense to me. After watching it for a month, I compiled a list of all the names of the companies the middlemen were buying from and took it to the vice president and general manager of the company, David Seltzer. I explained what I had been observing and asked him two questions: "Why don't *we* go to Europe and buy the sample shirts? And since I have the names of all the textile mills in Asia that the converters are buying from, why do we need them to purchase the fabric for us? Why don't we just set up appointments with each mill and buy directly, ourselves, and I will direct the design and color choices?" He looked at me and said, "Let me think about that and get back to you."

The next day he came in and said, "We're going to Europe and Asia." Sure enough, a few weeks later he and I went to Europe, where we bought a series of shirts to supplement our collection. I found an outside service to contract print different colors of our choice. Then we went to Asia: we had made appointments with various textile mills in Japan, Taiwan, and Korea, and we bought 75,000 yards of fabric on that trip and imported it directly to the United States. Five years later, we were purchasing 50 million yards a year, shipping it to our U.S. factories, and exporting to factories around the world. This gave us new insight into all our costs and saved the company millions of dollars. This cost/benefit and the exclusivity led us to become the second largest shirt company. This and many other smart corporate moves led us to overtake and acquire the number one shirt company, Arrow Shirts, in 2004. To this day, PVH, which was number three, is the largest shirt company in the world.

The point of this story is that *I didn't accept the norm*. Instead, I disrupted the system. I didn't like what was happening even though it was comfortable for everyone else in the company. I wanted to dig and figure out how this process could work better. Was there a more efficient way to operate? Was there a way we could learn more and be more in control? Was there an idea that we were missing here? Why did we need someone between us and the source? How many ways are there to get to the bottom line? I dug a little deeper and found a better way.

You need to do the same thing in your company. Don't accept the status quo even if everyone says, "That's just the way we do things around here." If you think you have a better way of doing something, suggest it. Maybe not on your first day on the job, maybe not even in the first month. But after you've built up some goodwill with your coworkers and your management, after they've learned a little about your work and your attitude and the results you achieve, you'll be in a more secure position of trust and they'll be more likely to listen to you, as David listened to me. Of course, you have to see it or find it, but even small things start to add up.

> Don't accept the status quo even if everyone says, "That's just the way we do things around here." If you think you have a better way of doing something, suggest it.

Every now and then, people tell me they can't suggest things in their companies because the response they get is, "Processes are too entrenched" or "That's always the way we've done things" or "We don't have the manpower or the know-how to do things differently" or "If it ain't broke, don't fix it." I suppose that does happen in some companies, although I don't see how those companies can survive, let alone thrive, if that's their mindset. I believe that if you're being brilliant or have a really great idea, you have to hope you're working for someone who sees that.

In my case, I was inquisitive. I was uncomfortable that we didn't have the information I thought we should have. I thought we were the experts and should start acting like experts. I hoped my boss would support my idea and try it. Fortunately for me and the company, he did see it right away. But if he hadn't, I probably would have gone above his head even at the risk of being fired. I realize that not everyone can take that risk, but I believed so strongly in my idea that I would have risked that. A more politically correct way to go about getting approval for a radical idea is to get someone else's opinion, since it's a stronger argument if you have other people supporting you. I firmly believe that no one can hold back the next great idea. In most companies your ideas will be welcome.

> I firmly believe that no one can hold back the next great idea.

Moreover, I was only 26 years old, yet I taught the system I developed to my direct report, Ted Sattler, who taught it to his direct report, Marcia Downs, who taught it to her direct reports, and so on. Even though I'm no longer there, the system still exists and still works at PVH. Today all companies have eliminated middlemen, and if there are textile converters, they are few and far between. Once in my life I was brilliant.

9

Life in the Fast Lane

Not long after my "brilliance," I was doing very well. I had been promoted to merchandise manager. I felt good about myself and my work, I was making good contributions to the company's overall success, and I was moving up the ladder. But I noticed that the people who were getting significant promotions all came from the sales side of the business* even for positions in merchandising management, product development management, and marketing management. This concerned me, because I thought, How does a great salesperson suddenly know all about advertising? What does a salesperson know about sourcing in Asia? Nothing, it seemed to me. Meanwhile, although I had moved up in my department, I was still working in merchandising, and it seemed I wasn't being considered for a higher-level managerial position. I asked for a one-on-one meeting with my boss.

I said, "I know the company likes me, and I have nothing but the highest accolades for the company. You guys have treated me well, and I love what I'm doing. However, it seems that every time there's a big job open, the person who gets that job has come out of sales. As a result, it doesn't look like merchandising is where I should be. I'm not sure I should stay with the company—or if I do, I clearly need to get into sales. I'm in the wrong spot, because you're not promoting anyone from this discipline."

---

*I'm sure this was happening in many companies, because the logic at the time was that the people closest to the end customer were the people with the greatest knowledge of the business. After all, they would call their retail clients, ask what was selling or working, and get a direct response. Today the heads of companies come from every discipline in the business environment. They can come from finance, merchandising, sales, or anywhere else.

He said, "Let me think about that, and I'll get back to you." He arranged for me to meet with the senior vice president of the company, Robert Solomon, who also knew me personally. By this time, I knew everyone in the company, and I had built up a lot of goodwill. A few days later, Mr. Solomon called me into his office to talk. He mentioned a few things I had done recently that had worked out well and said he was really happy with my work and my performance. Then he asked me about the conversation I had had with my boss, and I told him the same thing: "I love this company. I feel the company has treated me well and that I've done well for the company. But I'm watching what's going on, and it seems to me that I'm in the wrong space to become one of the heads of the company someday, and that's what I'd really like to do. I'd like to think I could be a major contributor, and being in the merchant side of the business, I don't see it happening."

He said, "Okay. Let's talk about that," and we began one of the most important conversations of my career. He asked me, "Mark, are you good at finance?" I said, "I understand finance. I relate well to it. I understand the economics of the company and what takes place. Yeah, I'm good at it." He asked, "Are you *great* at it?" I thought and said, "No, I'm not great at it."

Then he said, "Okay. Let's talk about sales. Are you good at selling?" I said, "I know how to present our products well, and I make good presentations." He didn't seem satisfied with that answer, because he asked me again, "But do you enjoy selling? Do you think you would be great at it?" I said, "I think I'd be good at it, and I think I would make a contribution. I believe I could do well at anything I put my mind to." Again he said, "I asked you if you'd be *great* at it." I answered truthfully: "No, that's not what I'd be great at."

Then he asked me, "Are you good at developing new products and new designs?" This time I said, "I'm great." He continued, "Are you a good merchant?" And I said, "No, I'm a *great* merchant." That was when he got to his point: "I'm going to stop right there, Mark. In this world, you're competing against the best. If you really want to talk to me about a big career, then you have to think about competing against the best, people who are *great* at what they do. For you to compete, it's not okay to be *good* at something to get to the top. If you go into finance and you're good, you're competing against *great*; if you transfer into sales, again, you'll be competing against sellers who are great, and if you're just good, you're not going to get to the top. But no question, you're great at product development, and that's what you should pursue, that's what you should be, because in this world if you're going to compete, you need to compete with what you're best at."

I have never forgotten that meeting or that insight. Learn everything else you can, respect every discipline that's out there, but if you're going to get to where you want to get, you have to be great at what you're going to do.

Then Mr. Solomon added the icing on the cake: "Mark, you're too important to the company for us to take you out of merchandising and move you into sales. In addition to what you're doing, I'm going to pair you with one of the key sales executives and charge him with the responsibility of teaching you the important components of sales." And that was what he did. I had my existing responsibility of heading up the product development area, but at the same time the head of marketing for the division, John Mueller, trained and taught me the other side of the business.

I worked hard to round out my merchandising knowledge by learning more of the analytical skills on the product development side. How much do you buy? When do you buy? How much do you buy? How do you keep track of it? What do you do with inventory that you don't sell? I needed to learn the inventory management side, and so I had about a year's worth of intense sales training and inventory management. At the end of that year, I was expecting to be promoted to vice president, general merchandise manager.

10

The Solid
Gold Rolex

When I first started doing business overseas, I had a lot to learn. What did I know about the world? Fortunately, I wanted to learn, but along the way I made at least one major gaffe.

My company had several licensees throughout South and Central America, and my first meeting was with a shirt-manufacturing company in a country that shall remain nameless.* It licensed the Van Heusen name for shirts to be sold in its territory. The owners of the company were also connected in government, and they had been doing business with my company for two generations and more than 50 years. For this meeting, the CEO "owner" of this company happened to be visiting New York, and so we met at our office to discuss several issues about our licensing arrangement.

The most troubling issue to me was that his company owed us $25,000. That may not seem like a lot of money to readers today, but it was significant, especially because his company had been in arrears for more than a year. I've never been tolerant of people who don't pay on time. I simply don't understand why it happens: if you're doing business with someone or some company and you've shaken hands on a deal, you should honor your obligations. I've never wavered in that belief.

However, I learned the hard way how to handle this problem. I was still rather young when I first met the patriarch of this family-owned business, and he was very charming, but he was also extremely intimidating. Because I was young and because I had just taken over the licensing division, I thought I knew everything and was an expert on

---

*To protect the innocent and the guilty.

licensing deals. When the CEO started talking about his country and how complicated business and the environment and the economy were, everything he said was going in one ear and out the other because all I could think of was that he owed us $25,000.

First, *don't be a wise guy,* and second, *understand the cultures you're involved with.*

I let him say his piece, and I took my time getting to what I thought was the biggest issue confronting us. Eventually I said, "You know, you owe us $25,000." He said, "Yes, I know, and we'll pay you eventually. Don't worry; we always do." I wasn't satisfied with that answer, though, and said, "I don't see any reason why you can't pay us now, especially since you're more than a year in arrears. You have a nice business here: you pay for electricity, you pay your employees. By the same token, you have to pay us." He wasn't upset by this comment, and he calmly responded, "We've always had an understanding that sometimes business is good and sometimes it's bad. So I need your company to bear with me right now."

I wasn't happy with that response either; to add insult to injury, while I was listening to him, I noticed he was wearing a solid gold Rolex. I said, "I'll tell you what: forget the payment. Give me your watch instead." I was making a joke, but I was also trying to make a point: clearly, this guy had money, so again, I didn't see why he should be late in paying our company what he owed us. I would have taken the watch and sold it. He didn't think my offer was funny at all: he looked at me with the meanest face I've ever seen in my life (even to this day) and said, "I think you should come visit my country. I'll give it to you there, but I don't know that you'll ever leave the country with it."

My blood ran cold, and I learned two very important lessons that day. First, *don't be a wise guy,* and second, *understand the cultures you're involved with.* Although I still think I was right and was entitled to get what he owed us, the way I went about it obviously insulted this guy, and he was angry. I think I'm funny, but I'm not sure I was funny when I said that. It was the wrong way to go about it. That was my entrée into international business. I realized that there are varying cultures, that the American style is different, and that much of the world is more reserved than Americans are. If you think you're funny, visit *The Late Show.* Business is business, and you must always stay in character and act appropriately.

11

Pearls of Wisdom

After the solid gold Rolex incident, I made it one of my goals to learn more about the protocols of doing business internationally. I believe it's essential to have a strong moral compass and to make sure you never, ever compromise yourself in any way when you're in business. Little did I know how soon I would encounter such a situation.

I was in Japan working with a Japanese trading company to develop a new product. I verified that the product had the properties needed to enable us and meet our requirements. I even flew in our engineers to test and verify the quality and properties. They gave me the go-ahead to buy the product. It was a multi-million-dollar contract for five years, and so it was an important deal for the company.

I started negotiations in the morning and concluded the deal with the trading company in the early evening. After the long day, I returned to my room in the hotel and saw that the message light was on. I called down to the front desk and was told I had a package. I asked for it to be delivered to my room. When I unwrapped it, expecting it to be business materials, there was a beautiful gift box from the company with which I had just concluded the deal. Inside the gift box was a necklace, a bracelet, and earrings of Mikimoto pearls—which are considered to be the highest-quality pearls in the world—along with a thank-you note

My first reaction was panic, because I knew it's not appropriate to accept gifts from anyone you do business with, but this was a problem I had not confronted before. I recognized early in my career that even the *perception* of impropriety is a problem. I had heard that businesspeople in some parts of the world were looser about the practice of gift giving, and I also knew, of course, that there were deals that were downright shady. I knew right from wrong! I would not have any part in anything that would even *appear* improper or inappropriate. Period.

I knew immediately that I must take action and ensure that my integrity was sacrosanct. In business (and in life), your word, your handshake, and your integrity are who you are. You cannot compromise. I called my boss in the New York office, who was the president of the company, and told him what had happened. I began with the good news: I had concluded the deal, we were getting everything we needed, and everybody was excited. Then I said I had a problem, and I told him about the pearls. I told him that I couldn't even imagine what they were worth but that they looked very expensive. I said, "I want you to know they sent me this gift, and I want you to know that I'm going to refuse it. I'm taking it down to the front desk, but I wanted you to know what happened so that no one in our company or any other company will ever be able to say that I accepted a gift inappropriately. I'm returning it now." Then the president of the company said, "That's very smart, very wise of you. I appreciate you calling, and I'm not surprised you did."

As soon as we hung up, I called my associate from our Hong Kong office, who was traveling with me, and said, "Get the Japanese trading company on the phone. Wake them up in their houses if you have to, but get them on the phone." Fortunately, the people I had been dealing with in Japan were still in their office, and I spoke to the American representative with whom I had negotiated the deal. I said, "I can't accept this: it's a very nice gesture, but you need to come pick this up." He tried to make light of it by saying, "But it's just our way of saying thank you." I said, "I'll tell you how you say thank you to me: you deliver everything you promised, on time. But I cannot accept a gift. That is not business." He said, "We are in Japan, and gifting is an accepted part of doing business." I told him, "I am an American, and gifting is not part of our business or our culture, and you should know better!" Case closed. Emphatically, I told him, "I am not accepting this gift, so you need to have someone from your office pick it up at the front desk. Otherwise, one of the young ladies at the front desk of this hotel will look very beautiful in a set of Mikimoto pearl jewelry." I hung up and took the pearls down to the front desk.

This incident is important because I truly believe that you should *never accept anything from anyone.* If you do, you become beholden to that person. And even if you aren't actually beholden, that person owns you. You must be above reproach at any level in a company and especially at the most senior levels. This keeps you objective and free of any entanglements, and it allows you to base decisions on what's right for your company, not what might be right for you personally. Trust me, this is perhaps even more important: when you put your head on your pillow at night, you can sleep soundly.

Some people might wonder, What constitutes a gift? I believe flowers are an acceptable gift from a business associate, because even though they can be expensive, it's a socially acceptable way of showing someone that you appreciate what he or she has done but it doesn't obligate that person in any way. Also, the flowers are displayed for all to enjoy.

> You must be above reproach at any level in a company and especially at the most senior levels.

With respect to business lunches and dinners, there are some very big companies that make it clear that they cannot accept a supplier paying the bill for a meal; because of the size and scope of their business, it may appear that the company is making decisions on the basis of those shared meals. Personally, I don't subscribe to that, although I do believe that when you have lunch or dinner with someone, there needs to be a specific business purpose for that lunch and it shouldn't be just a social event. However, if you're the type of person who might be compromised by a meal, I suggest that you pay your own way so that you won't be tempted.

I continue to be surprised at how many people don't understand or accept this idea, and I think it's a really important lesson to learn. I've known buyers who have even asked for samples of merchandise, which is a poor business practice. They may think they're trying to show the designer or the vendor how much they like the merchandise; still, that's not a good way to do business. You should not accept anything free from anyone. There are cases, for example, in which a vendor may want a woman to wear-test a dress or a man to wear-test a suit. When they give an item like this to you, make sure to write a detailed report on that product. You need to be above reproach, and as I explained above, even the appearance of impropriety is a problem in my view. That's my personal policy, and I recommend it to everyone reading this book. These are my pearls of wisdom and part of your personal business success manual.

12

You Can't Always Get What You Want

Until now, I've written mostly about my early career successes. I was on a roll. Everything I touched worked. Even though I was young, I was in control.

But I had to learn the hard way that it's not only what you do right that gets you to the top; it's how you deal with *disappointment*. You don't get the job or the raise or the promotion that you want. The person you're competing with gets the job you hoped you would get. There are many disappointments in everyone's career, no matter how successful a person appears to be. The key to success is how you deal with those disappointments.

First, you have to understand what your company is trying to accomplish. The most you can expect from any company is to be treated fairly. If that's happening, you need to recognize it and live to fight another day. You can't always get what you want, and when your company or your boss says no to you, your disappointment will build your character and make you a better person, but that will happen only if you let it. You need to think about who you are. Are you interested in doing what's right? Are you focused on the correct values? Those values will reflect on your decisions. And yes, how do you manage disappointment? Your company is not a monster.

One of the major reasons I believe I have been successful in my career is that I dealt with my disappointments the right way.

I had been given increasing responsibilities all along, moving up from assistant designer to men's fashion director and marketing director. Although that was six positions in six years—a record that any other person would have been thrilled with—I wanted and expected more for myself. I wanted to become a vice president. I believed I deserved it, and I believed I was ready for the next challenge and the next level up. I thought the senior managers at my company, who would be making that decision, agreed with me. Little did I know what was about to happen.

I was in Europe on business with Helen Katz, a colleague from product development. I've known Helen my entire career, and I value her friendship to this day, not only because she's smart, talented, and hardworking but also because she saved me from myself on that trip. We were in Nuremberg and had completed a whirlwind shopping tour for technical design. We had finished an early dinner when we received a message to call the New York office, and when we did, there were three people on the phone: Chuck Smith, the president of the company; the executive vice president; and John, one of the regional sales managers. They said they had great news. First, they announced that the regional sales manager on the call had been promoted to vice president and general manager over our division. Second, another merchandise executive who held the same position I did—my archcompetitor—had been promoted to VP. Third, another merchandiser who was junior to me had been promoted to my level. As I listened to this, I thought to myself, This is "great news"? Not to me, it isn't.

So I asked them, "But what about *me*?"

"What do you mean, what about you?" the president asked.

I said, "Well, you told me you had great news, and all these other people were promoted, but I didn't hear anything about me." After that, they were quiet for a minute, and then the president said, "Well, you'll continue doing what you're doing, but you'll be working for John (a sales executive) now. We think you'll get a great education because John has a lot to offer."

I took a moment to breathe, and then I lost my cool and said, "Are you out of your f***ing mind? You asked me to call you at eight at night and this is what you f***ing have to say to me? I can't believe you're not promoting me. I can't believe this sh*t."

I don't usually curse or use vulgarity at work or anywhere else for that matter, but I was so taken aback by their "great news" that I simply unleashed this string of four-letter words. When I was finished, the president of the company said to me, "Mark, if that's how you feel, be on the next plane home tomorrow and we'll talk about it when you return." And he hung up.

I was still really angry. I remember clearly what happened next. Helen was shocked and said, "Mark, do you realize you just resigned from the company without even talking to your wife?" I said, "What are you talking about? I didn't resign!" She said, "Yes, you did. That's what they think you just did. If you didn't resign, they're firing you." Now *I* was shocked, and I realized she was right. Thirty seconds later, I called back. John answered, and I immediately apologized and tried to explain why I had reacted so offensively and unprofessionally: "I had high hopes: I thought I would also be moving up, but the people you've promoted are great at their jobs. I understand why you promoted them, and I'm really happy for them. And I'm very sorry for what I said." I groveled!

I was fortunate in a lot of ways that night—first, because Helen was there to help me dig myself out of the hole I had dug. When you're in a hole, the first rule is to stop digging. I'm incredibly grateful, and I've never forgotten what she did for me that day.

Second, I called back immediately because the three of them were still in the president's office; therefore, I was able to apologize right away. I don't know what would have happened if I had waited any longer. I probably would have been fired, which would have made me miserable, because I really loved my work at that company.

Third, I had a lot of goodwill going for me. I truly believe I would have lost my job if not for my track record of working so hard and doing so well for all the years leading up to this unfortunate phone call. When I called back and apologized, John said, "Look, Mark, I'm not sure why you're upset, but finish your trip. Do what you've got to do, then come back here. I really need you, and we're going to work well together. " He didn't want to lose me, either. He needed me to be successful. We all need good people.

I recognize that there was also a lot of good luck working in my favor that night. But even more important than luck, I learned a very valuable lesson about what not to do when you're disappointed in your career. Obviously, don't swear at the president of your company. But more important, remember that this is *business*; these are not your friends or family. You have to control your emotions. You need to understand that the company comes first and you deserve only to be treated fairly.

I ate a lot of crow for about a year afterward: whenever I attended meetings with the three people who were on the call that night, there came a point when they asked me—only me, not the 10 other people in the room—to leave the meeting so they could discuss issues they didn't want me to be involved with. I received no raise that year. It was no fun being in the doghouse. I needed to rebuild their respect. I lost my cool, and when you lose that, you can lose everything. I toughed it out, but it took a long time before I was completely back in their good graces.

> You have to control your emotions. You need to understand that the company comes first and you deserve only to be treated fairly.

I have not had a straight line to a successful career (more on that later). But I assure you that whatever success I have had in large measure comes from that night in Nuremberg. You need to learn to control your emotions, to take all emotion out of any situation. Let disappointments fuel your desire to prove your worth. If you deserve to win, you will. Never forget: companies need people. They thrive on excellence. Demonstrate excellence and you can get to where you want to be. Use disappointments to intensify your determination.

The big lesson I learned was that you've got to be level-headed and you need to always consider the company's position—what's best for the company even if it's not what's best for you.

Even today, 30 years after this happened, I still tell that to people. Today I'm in the other position (most of the time): as CEO, the most I'm responsible for is to treat my company's employees fairly whether I'm deciding on raises, promotions, or bonuses. Moreover, this concept applies to many aspects of life because most of us face so many disappointments and so many setbacks, but what's important is how you deal with them to get ahead. Ever since that night, any time I had a setback in my career, it was a trigger to identify a new goal and a new mountain to climb. I believe that's why I have the position I have today—not because I'm smart but because of the way I dealt with disappointment.

I don't believe there are any flukes in business. I believe people get ahead because they deserve to. Some people make it farther than they should, but that catches up to them eventually. In my case, when I look back on that situation, I ask myself, "Do the people who were promoted have talent?" and "Why did they get this promotion instead of me?" I don't have to like the decisions and don't have to agree with them, but I need to understand why they were made.

Then you need to decide how you're going to deal with each disappointment. Sometimes you'll make the right move; other times you'll make the wrong move. The most important thing is to have a level head and always consider whether the company is being fair. You have to make a decision right then and there: Are you going to let it affect you, or are you going to use it as motivation to get ahead? Okay, they don't think I'm good enough for this? I'm going to show them why they're wrong! After I was passed over for that promotion, I worked even harder to learn everything I could about my company's business.

13

One Step Forward, Two Steps Back

Not long after the company decided to train me in sales and marketing, I saw that I needed to know much more than that. I completely understood (better than anyone else in the company) what it cost to manufacture fabric and shirts and the impact those costs had on the price point and the competition. I knew how to create merchandise and how to price it, and I had presented our merchandise to every retailer in the country. But I didn't understand the overall financial side of the business. I didn't see how all the financial elements fit together, how we made money, or how a company decides what to invest in or not.

Unfortunately, this also became apparent to my company, to my detriment. I was about 30 years old, and I was traveling in Taiwan to visit a factory with the senior vice president, who was my boss's boss. He respected me and my capabilities in various aspects of the business, but his favorite person at my level—with whom I was competing for promotions—had also been mentored on the financial side. I happened to ask the SVP a question that I would not have needed to ask if I had been trained properly in the financials. I knew I had asked the wrong question at the wrong time when the SVP asked me, "You don't *know* that?" He was astounded, and at that moment I watched my career go backward two years.

He realized I hadn't been trained in the disciplines I should have been trained in to take the next step in my career. Meanwhile, two of my competitors were promoted before I was because they had been trained. (This is why I was left behind when the announcements were made in Nuremberg about other people's promotions.) Even worse, it became clear that if my lack of understanding in the financial area wasn't rectified, I was finished moving up the ladder.

I hadn't been trained in financials because I was so good at what I was doing: I was a really talented designer. My competitors weren't: their products weren't as exciting as mine. However, they knew the math and I didn't.

I talked to my bosses and told them I needed to learn the financial side of the business. Fortunately, they agreed and arranged for me to learn what I needed to know. They moved me into a position for six months in which I worked for someone who understood all the merchandising components of the business: how to plan, how to intake merchandise into inventory, when to sell it, what not to do. And I learned all the financials—if you sell 1,000 shirts at a 50 percent markup and you sell 500 shirts at a 40 percent markup, you have 300 shirts that didn't sell, and where does that leave you? Are you meeting your financial plan or not? I spent six months to a year learning that under the tutelage of a financial expert and with a really talented group.

Then, at the end of that year, they made me the manager of everyone in that group. I became the general merchandising manager (GMM) of the entire shirt division because no one could compete with me from a creative point of view, and now that I had learned the financials, no one could compete with me in terms of my understanding of costs and the way to bring products into the country. Importing is an important part of the fashion industry, and that's essentially what VPs and GMMs do in department stores. Once I learned the numbers, there was no stopping me.

I was determined to learn the financial side even if my company hadn't arranged for me to learn it on the job, even if I had to learn it on my own time. That's how important I knew this education was to my future advancement. I could have taken classes in retail math. I knew I needed to understand how our company managed its inventory and its financials, how it projected its numbers, how it reported on those projections, and how it tracked performance. If they hadn't provided that training for me, I would have known it was time to leave the company. And if I had had the financial wherewithal to do it at the time (and I did), I would have taken that risk.

However, I was confident in my ability and in the knowledge that the company wanted me to succeed and continue to advance. I believe that the more senior a person is, the more willing he or she is to help you when you ask for it. That doesn't mean there isn't politics or golden boys (or golden gals), but if you believe you can do more, you have to make that happen for yourself. You might not do it right away because not everything happens instantly, but you have to keep your eyes open for opportunities and push yourself to learn what you need to know.

Some people might think they don't have the time or energy to learn a new discipline while they're working at what is probably an already demanding job. In terms of time, I admit first and foremost that I wouldn't have been as successful if I didn't have the support of my wife. She is and always has been a great partner to me, and she understood what I was trying to achieve. I made time for her and my two sons, Jarrod and Jesse, and I'm proud to say I found a balance between my work and my family. I made it a priority to do that because I didn't want to look back on my life and say that I was not a good father or that I missed my boys' childhood. And some of the happiest days of my life were spent watching my sons play high school sports. I wouldn't have missed that for any promotion.

I believe energy is an important component to being successful. More important than energy is whether you're excited by and interested in your business. You have to like what you're doing. This relates to my basic belief that *work is work if it's work*. If work is work, you can't enjoy yourself, but I never felt that work was work.

To this day, I'll work as hard as anyone because I'm motivated or because I enjoy what I'm doing. If you're not happy with what you're doing, you're going to have a difficult work life, and I think there's nothing worse than that. You have to find something that makes you happy.

Admittedly, I was fortunate not only because I was hardworking, ambitious, and motivated but because the company liked me and rewarded me with the education and training I needed. If that hadn't happened, I would have had to take a hard look at myself and consider that maybe I had reached the place in my career where I was supposed to be. Not everyone is destined to become the president or CEO of a company. If that had been the case, I would have learned to make the most of what I had and enjoy what I was doing because I would have realized that that was where I belonged.

The other side of the coin is that everyone has choices. Success depends on the way you package yourself (I'll talk more about that in a later chapter), what people think of you, and your innate capabilities. If you believe sincerely that you're capable of more, you have to convince your company that you can do more or look outside your company to figure out how to do that.

If you decide to join another company, you can reboot yourself. You can be whoever you want. Maybe you made mistakes in the way you presented yourself. Maybe you made some poor business decisions. Maybe you didn't talk to or interact with people appropriately. Whatever you think you did wrong at a previous company, you can correct when you move to a new company. Nobody knows you, and so you can make a fresh start. Take the best of what you learned and leave behind any baggage that's holding you back. There's always another job out there, and if your company doesn't think you're the best at what you do, another company may think you are. You need to learn what you need to know to succeed, and you need to decide if the company you're working for will help you or if you need to help yourself.

14

Packaging Yourself Is as Important as Packaging Your Products

P art of getting what you want is what you do before you even know you want it. Learning how to present and package yourself is critical to your success. Although it shouldn't matter what you look or sound like, it does. Remember, you're in business, and the people you meet and work with are not your friends; they are business associates. That's a big difference. As a former designer, marketer, and product developer, I'm convinced that most people really, truly don't know how to look their best, and it's important that you know that.

First, you need to know who you're working for. If you work for an investment bank, look at how the people you work with are dressed. I assure you that each and every one, from the boss on down, cares a great deal about the image he or she is presenting. They want to look like they're successful. All the men will have the best suits, the best shirts, the best ties, and the best color coordination possible. All the women will wear the best suits or the most sophisticated and elegant dresses, and they will be completely covered; they will not be showing a lot of skin. They will carry luxury handbags, briefcases, and shoes because investment bankers need to signal that they know what to do with money; if they spend their own money wisely, that indicates that they also know how to invest your money.

In contrast, if you work for a high-tech company, you face different circumstances. You want to show that you're cutting edge, that you know what the next thing will be, and that you're cool. You don't have to shave every day for work; as a matter of fact, it may be a benefit if you're disheveled, because you'll be signaling that you're so caught up in the next technology that you don't have time to think about what you're wearing. Wherever you work, you need to understand the culture of your company and know the right signals to send.

At one of the divisions I ran, we instituted casual Friday, and the CFO of that division showed up unshaven, wearing torn jeans and a T-shirt. When I saw that, I said, "You're kidding, right? You're the chief financial officer." He said, "Yeah, but it's casual Friday." I said, "Casual Friday doesn't mean that competition in the workplace disappears with the removal of your jacket and tie. You're still the CFO. You're supposed to look good because you're sending a signal to everyone else. You don't have to wear a suit and tie on Fridays, but you can't come to work looking like this."

When casual Fridays were introduced, there was tremendous confusion (there still is) about how to dress appropriately: many people couldn't figure out what constitutes casual clothing that's not sloppy or too informal. Casual Friday does not mean it's appropriate to wear torn jeans, flip-flops, paint-stained T-shirts, sweatpants, or anything else you might wear when you're cleaning your house, putting up drywall, buying groceries, or hanging out in your neighbor's backyard. You need to think about what image you want to convey to others—even to your coworkers, even if you're not meeting with the public or with customers or suppliers. The way you dress and look is very important.

There are plenty of real-life consultants who can help you with the way you dress and even the way you speak and the way you walk. If you can't afford to pay an image consultant, it's important to look to your role models and emulate the way they dress, act, and speak. There's an old saying: Don't dress for the job you have; dress for the job you want. First of all, you have to want to improve. Then you have to take a really critical look at yourself in the mirror and ask, "What do I really want to achieve?" and "Do I have what it takes to get there?"

You don't need to be the handsomest or most beautiful person in the world, because there are other ways to get ahead. It's not your *looks* that matter; it's the way you carry and present yourself, and that includes the way you speak. Before any important meeting, it's critical to think about what you want to convey and how you want to convey it and to appear in control of the events that are surrounding you even though sometimes those events may seem overwhelming. Also, *every* meeting is important if you are with someone who's senior to you. The way I presented my case was and still is often the significant factor in getting "permission" or buy-in on my ideas.

I had been with PVH for only a few weeks when I was first inspired to learn how to speak well to a large group of people. The company had an off-site meeting with everyone in the New York office, and the president of the company, Mr. Stanley Gillette, walked up to the podium and made a state-of-the-union speech in which he described what was going on in the company. He was very distinguished-looking, and he spoke more eloquently than anyone I had ever met. Remember, I had just gotten out of the concrete jungle of Brooklyn, where I would have never met anyone like this, not in a million years.

He spoke without any notes for an hour. I watched and listened to him attentively, because I couldn't believe what I was seeing. And I made up my mind that I was going to learn how to do that. I didn't know how, I didn't know when, but I was going to do that.

Today I can speak for an hour without any notes, perhaps not as eloquently, but I can certainly hold my own. I learned how to do that by watching people speak and preparing exhaustively every time I give a speech. People come up to me afterward and say, "Wow, that was great. You made it look so easy." But they have no idea how much work and preparation went into that speech. They don't know how many times I've written it, tweaked it, and practiced it while standing at a podium or in front of a mirror, holding my notes but not looking down at them. I practice not only the content but the organization and sequence of information, the way it flows, even the pacing. I do all this so that by the time I'm in front of an audience, it *will* look easy. Just as the harder I work, the luckier I get, in this case, the harder I work, the easier it looks.

I want to speak with authority so that people will recognize that I know what I'm talking about. I want to make sure I know my subject matter thoroughly because there are always questions, and I make very few speeches in which I don't include a question-and-answer period. That is a very bold thing to do if you're not prepared or don't know the subject matter.

The key to learning anything is first and foremost to decide what you want to learn. In my case, I wanted to learn how to speak comfortably in front of an audience, without notes. Next, find a standard: someone who has the skill you want to have, whom you can emulate. I was fortunate to be surrounded by executives who knew how to speak well. Stanley Gillette was not the only one I emulated. Larry Phillips, the grandson of the founder of PVH, was also an amazing speaker. He was smart as a whip and Princeton-educated, and he had a fantastic ability to speak extemporaneously (or what *appeared* to be extemporaneously). Many people in the company dreaded speaking after Larry Phillips because he was such a tough act to follow. I often had to follow him, but I didn't dread it because first, I wanted to learn how to speak well; second, I had great mentors to watch and emulate; third, I focused on preparing for each speech; and fourth, I practiced and practiced and practiced.

> The way you convince people has a lot to do with the way you present and the way you prepare.

To this day, I believe in the power of a great presentation. I work with people on my team all the time to help them improve their presentation skills because they're so critical. I make sure that everyone who makes presentations to our board of directors or senior executives has every *i* dotted and every *t* crossed. It's not enough to have all the right information; in addition, you need to ensure that all the information you present is directly relevant, organized in the best possible way, and as succinct as it can be so that your audience (in this case the board) can easily understand what you're trying to convey, which will lead them to support whatever you're proposing. The way you convince people has a lot to do with the way you present and the way you prepare.

How will you package yourself for your next promotion?

15

Maybe Twice
in My Career
I Was Brilliant

At 34 years old, I was divisional president of the Van Heusen Company. I had always been involved in the marketing of the companies and the brands I worked with, but now I was responsible for advertising all the brands in the company. As a young man, I learned from our head of advertising and one of my great collaborators, Henry Justus, that "the number one rule of marketing and advertising is to break through the clutter." The other important idea I've always kept in mind is paraphrased from the legendary retailer John Wanamaker: I know 50 percent of my advertising works; I just don't know which 50 percent.

Marketing is the sum total of everything you do to build your brands. Everyone who has a product is constantly thinking, What can I do to make my brand more important? What can I do to make my brand more valuable? What can I do to make my brand demand a higher price point? What can I do to make sure my brand lasts the test of time? What can I do to make sure my brand is the chosen brand against my competitor? How do I make sure I don't wake up one day and be irrelevant? These are the things marketers worry about.

Successful marketing depends on understanding your customers. At Phillips-Van Heusen we sold men's clothes, and so we marketed and advertised to men. Seems obvious, right? Yet when I took over advertising for the company and started to study advertising and marketing trends, I began to wonder if that really was the best approach. I learned what our company had historically been spending on television advertising and print advertising as well as other media. I also noticed that the world of fashion, especially luxury fashion, was spending more and more on print advertising in magazines and newspapers. Print ads were lasting: you could stare at the page, and a magazine had a long shelf life, being passed from person to person. First we made a decision: no more TV unless there was some special event. All the important players in our business were in magazines.

As I made this decision, I realized I needed more information. Henry and I decided we should meet with every magazine and newspaper publisher. We met not only with the publishers of men's magazines but, more important, with the publishers of *Vogue, Vanity Fair, Elle, Harper's Bazaar*, and every other major women's magazine. During the course of those meetings, I started to think about where we were spending our advertising dollars and who we were trying to reach with our advertisements. I discovered that about 70 percent* of men's shirts were purchased or purchase-influenced by women. Yet all the men's clothing designers and manufacturers were spending their advertising money in men's magazines or in the sports section of newspapers because we all thought that was what our customers were reading.

One day, I was talking to Ron Galotti, who was then the publisher of *Vogue*, and I suddenly realized that most of my customers were women but I was putting all my advertising in men's publications. Right then and there, I decided to spend the entire season's marketing money in women's magazines only. This was the first time anyone working in a men's venue spent the entirety of the budget on women's magazines, but it worked. This decision in part led to the first billion-dollar year for the company.

Also, I believe our decision influenced many other companies that now advertise in women's magazines, whereas they hadn't before. People started to realize that their customers—the actual buyers of their products—weren't always the end users of their products. That may seem obvious now, but at the time it was a fresh idea. In fact, I won a Top 100 award from *Advertising Age* for doing something so creative and out of the box.

Another benefit of our decision to advertise in women's magazines was that every women's magazine started courting our business, and the men's magazines we had stopped advertising in became even

---

*I don't recall the exact number; this is an estimate.

hungrier for our business. As a result, we were offered better prices for our advertising, and many publications were competing for our business. If we advertised in one women's magazine but not another, the other one pursued us. That changed the whole price matrix for us in terms of buying media. That's capitalism at its best.

Advertising is part art, part science, and part instinct. In this situation, I was motivated partly by instinct, but I also had some science—in terms of statistics—to back me up. It didn't just come out of left field, but my instinct told me this was a way to break through the clutter and get our products noticed.

You need to have the data to back up your difficult decisions, and you have to be in a position to defend them; at the same time, you need to have the courage of your convictions. You can't learn everything just by reading a book—not even this one. Much of what gets done in life comes from instinct, so don't be afraid of it.

> People started to realize that their customers—the actual buyers of their products—weren't always the end users of their products.

16

Who Wants to Be a Millionaire?

There were many fans of the TV show *Who Wants to Be a Millionaire?*, which was popular at the time—not only popular, a phenomenon. It was hosted then by Regis Philbin, who started wearing dark-colored shirts and matching ties on every show. Suddenly, that combination became very popular: nobody had ever seen that look before, he looked terrific every evening, and he started a new trend in men's fashion. Someone (I don't remember who) proposed offering Regis a deal to develop a line of shirts (made by us) and ties (made by our licensee) for him. The key to this type of arrangement is a master licensor with clout. In this case, it was to be our own company: the shirts were the key because the ties needed the shirts.

I've always been skeptical about gimmicks in fashion because I'm concerned they won't stand the test of time, but the vice chairman of the company, Allen Sirkin, thought the idea was worth exploring. I asked how much he thought we could sell of such a product line, and he said, "I think we could do between 100,000 and 200,000 dozen shirts a year for the next few years." That was a lot of shirts—and also a lot of money—if he was right: a potential $25 million. The vice chairman overseeing the shirt division had a strong track record; he knew how to develop a product line, and he knew how many and which stores would sell this type of product. He convinced me we had a shot at succeeding at this, and so I decided to approach Regis and see if I could negotiate a deal.

We found out who Regis's agent was—Jim Griffin with William Morris Agency (now retired)—and Lee Terrill, division president, and I went to see him. Jim had already spoken to Regis about what we were interested in doing, and he told us, "Regis is interested, but it will be $1 million on signing and $1 million a year for the next two years." That was pretty big money by anyone's standard, and I told him I'd think about it.

Frankly, I didn't know how we were going to come up with $3 million. I wasn't at all sure I was prepared to invest that kind of money just because our shirt division was confident it could sell Regis Philbin shirts. I came up with an idea. I met with Allen and his associates and said, "We're going to start a bidding war for the ties. We're going to create a situation where the ties are bigger than the shirts. We think they can sell more ties, because the ties are one-third or one-half the price of the shirts. Also, because men could buy anybody's solid-color shirts, we'll package some shirts and ties together, because I think the tie part of the deal is huge."

We called in the three largest American tie companies and asked them what they could do, and I started a bidding war. I really wanted to do the deal with the tie company that was our licensee on other products, and so I told each tie company that the only way it could get the deal was if we split all the royalties and that we needed to offer some big guarantees to William Morris, which was representing Regis. I told them, "I need $1 million from you on signing and a guarantee of $1 million a year for two years, and if you can come up with that, I'll stop the bidding war and the deal is yours."

Our licensee came back to us the next day and guaranteed $1 million on signing and $1 million a year for the next two years. In other words, I got the shirts for free. We still paid a royalty for every shirt we sold. But I found a way to do this deal, which I didn't have my full heart in because it was risky, I didn't think it was good for the long term, and after hearing Regis's terms, it wasn't so simple, either. I agreed to do the license with Regis, but the negotiation with the tie company was what allowed us to go forward, because we had all the leverage. And in the end everybody made money.

Unfortunately, the product line lasted only about two years. That's what fashion is about, after all: at some point in time things fade. The *Millionaire* show started to wane. Also, every other company started making dark-colored shirts, and so we lost our first-to-market advantage and the market was flooded with competition. Consumers didn't need to buy our shirts even though we were packaging them with matching ties.

Still, it was a great deal while it lasted. We held a joint press conference hosted by me and Regis to announce this fashion collaboration.

It was held at the Four Seasons because Regis preferred that restaurant and we were to have lunch afterward. The press coverage was extraordinary. Every news outlet was there: local and national newspapers and all the TV networks and cable stations. They all covered it, and over the next few days it ran on and on.

Eventually, two unexpected things happened as a result of this press conference. The first happened about a year later: Regis wrote a book that mentioned the wonderful lunch we had afterward. He also pointed out that in our enthusiasm, we had stiffed him for the bill. Very funny.

The second thing that happened was not so funny but revealed interesting company politics. The Monday after the press conference, Bruce asked me into his office. He said he'd held a dinner party in his house on Saturday night and everyone who was there had seen the Regis coverage. His guests kept inquiring, "I thought *you* were the president of the company. Who's this guy Mark Weber with Regis?" Bruce said he and his wife were embarrassed, and therefore he would handle any future press coverage opportunities for the company. My role as front man was back-burnered for a time. Once again, human nature reared its head.

17

Negotiating with the Master

A few years later. another interesting licensing deal came our way. Donald Trump wanted to expand his brand into consumer goods and felt he could be successful in men's apparel. He cleverly forged a relationship with Terry Lundgren, the hands-on CEO of one of the largest and best American retailers, Macy's, which was very interested in supporting him if he could find partners who would produce Donald Trump products. Trump wanted to "license" his brand for men's clothing—suits, shirts, ties, and the like—because he believed he would be very successful at this given the fact that he was always wearing a suit on *The Apprentice* TV show.

One day the licensing director of Trump's organization called the licensing department in my company. We met with them, and the first question I asked myself was, Do I need this? The answer was no: my company could do very well without having the Donald Trump product in our stable. The second question was, Am I concerned that someone else will get it? Again the answer was no: I didn't think his brand would be a serious competitive threat to our product lines. Also, I had concerns that his brand wouldn't last the test of time, because the Regis line hadn't.

We were pleased with our association with Regis—he is a great, classy guy—and the license had brought us an outstanding publicity benefit by tapping into the TV audience. And both Regis and my company made a lot of money. But in the end, it wasn't our core brand. It was an ancillary brand that had a great run while it lasted, but it came and went fairly quickly. Therefore, I felt that licensing Donald Trump's name was not something we wanted to go forward with, and I decided to pass.

Then I got a call from Donald Trump's office saying he wanted to come see me personally. I said "yeah, sure" because I thought they were kidding. The next day Donald Trump and two of his staff members were sitting in my conference room, discussing Donald Trump shirts. He was bigger than life. He is one of the most interesting people I've ever met. I can't imagine anyone with a stronger desire to be successful.

He was very cordial and very professional. He began by explaining why he wanted this deal: menswear would be an important component of his brand. He felt that men would relate to products with his name and brand and that there was a lot of money to be made—for both of our companies. Don't forget, it was Donald Trump. I listened to what he had to say, but then I reiterated what our licensing department had already conveyed to him: I didn't need to license his name (for the reasons described above), and although I thought it was a clever idea and believed he could be successful, I didn't think it was right for us.

We knew he had a very strong following of young guys who admired him because he is a billionaire who carries himself well and because of the way he delivered "You're fired" at the end of every episode of *The Apprentice*. Some people love him and some people don't, but I think he's interesting to everyone. I was and continue to be a fan and admirer.

Interestingly, the more I told him no, the harder he pushed. The more we weren't interested, the more he pressed. The more we pushed back, the more he wanted to do this deal. At one point he said to me, "I've never met anyone as tough as you," and I said, "It's not that I'm tough. I just don't need this deal." Then I told him about how we had licensed Regis Philbin's name for a line of shirts and it hadn't stood the test of time. I thought licensing Trump's brand would have the same result that licensing Regis Philbin's had: it wouldn't be very successful for very long.

Mr. Trump didn't accept that argument. He said, "Regis Philbin is my dear, dear friend. I love him. What he does is amazing: there's no one more comfortable on TV than he is, no one more successful, but he's not building a brand. He's an amazing entertainer; *I'm* a brand. I want to be affiliated with the best. I'm told your company is the best at shirts. Moreover, I'll promise you one thing: the Donald Trump brand is going to live on. Doing this deal means more to me than you know. Everywhere I go, I establish the highest quality, the best workmanship, the best design I possibly can, and I'm not in this for the short term.

Building my brand matters a great deal to me. I don't just put my name on buildings or golf courses. I do it with the greatest integrity. I want the *best* buildings and the *best* golf courses. I don't cut corners. In fact, I improve everything I touch, and that's what I want you to keep in mind: if you agree to do this, I'll go anywhere, I'll talk to anyone, and I'll do everything I can to make this product line successful."

He made such a compelling case and he was so believable that we agreed to sign a license for Donald Trump shirts and ties, and it was fascinating to watch how he delivered on his promise. He did many great things to market his clothing line, but one in particular convinced me how driven a businessman he was

We agreed to build a Donald Trump showroom in our building. It was a small showroom, maybe 20 by 20 feet, but it was dedicated to his brand: it was only Donald Trump shirts and ties and some suits he had licensed to round out the collection and make it look complete. Then the marketing people in my company decided to have a ribbon-cutting ceremony. We invited about 150 of our own people who wanted to meet Trump, we called one reporter from *Women's Wear Daily*, and we had our own photographer to take pictures of our people with him. Donald came with his licensing team and his wife, Melania, and they were dressed to the nines. He was incredibly gracious and friendly: he shook hands, signed autographs, and posed for pictures with anyone and everyone who asked. As I watched him doing all this, I thought to myself, What is he doing here? This is an internal event, a showroom in my facility, not even in a retail store, and he's greeting all our people. So I whispered in his ear, "Donald, why are you doing this?" And he looked straight at me and said, "Because I want to win, and I'll do whatever it takes to win."

To make a long story short, 10 years later, the Donald Trump clothing line is still in every Macy's. He was right: it did stand the test of time. You don't stay if you are not relevant. It was a great deal for us to make, and I'm glad we worked with him.* If you were to put a picture above the words "will to succeed," it would be Donald Trump's.

---

*As a side note, he also proved to be a stand-up guy personally. He kept in touch with me after I was let go from PVH and rumors about me were circulating in the press. Every time something was written about me, he sent me a copy of the article on which he had written things such as "Get 'em, kid" or "Don't let them get you down" or "Bigger than ever." It was very nice to know he supported me, and I think he's a good man in that regard.

18

Run Away!

We had been successful with the Regis Philbin and Donald Trump licensing deals and many others, but that doesn't mean we were always successful either in licensing or in acquisition deals. In fact, sometimes the best deal is the one you walk away from.

When I was at PVH, a company called Crystal Brands was for sale because it was going through bankruptcy. Crystal Brands manufactured and sold sportswear, costume jewelry, and accessories, with brands including Izod, Gant, and Monet. The Monet business was more than $100 million, with a 21 percent share of the costume jewelry market, which is a very dynamic market share. Its products were distributed throughout the United States in some of the finest stores: anyone who sold costume jewelry carried Monet. Although we didn't really know anything about costume jewelry, we were enamored with Monet's market share and profit margins, and so the CEO of PVH and the team decided to move full speed ahead to buy the entirety of the Crystal Brands Company, including Monet. At that time, the company was being sold in parts, and although we wanted all the parts, Monet was the first one up for sale. I was vice chair of PVH, and if we bought Crystal Brands, I would be responsible for running its various companies, as I did with all our acquisitions.

The banks arranged for us to meet as many people as possible: the existing management as well as former executives who had been in the Monet business. Still, the CEO made it clear that it was my responsibility to feel comfortable with this purchase if it went through. I remember him saying to me, "Mark, this is going to be your acquisition. You're going to have to run these companies—all of them—so you need to tell me whether or not you have concerns, understand the risks, and then recommend whether or not we should do this deal." He as CEO was ultimately responsible, but this was his way of applying pressure to ensure that I was confident in the decision.

Of course, whenever we purchased a company, we brought in a group of people with experience in different disciplines to do due diligence on all aspects of the company we were considering acquiring: warehousing, manufacturing, information technology, design, public relations, sales, marketing, advertising, and so forth. For several months, this team explored very closely every aspect of Crystal Brands and its various businesses and brands.

Unfortunately, what we didn't realize until it was almost too late was that we were succumbing to groupthink, which happens frequently when you put together a group of people to accomplish a mission. Groupthink often takes over when people are so committed to making something happen that they don't watch out for any red flags that might come up: they're so keen on finding a way to make everything work that they talk themselves into simply accomplishing the mission. In this case, everybody on the due diligence team knew that our chairman and we, the senior management team, wanted to do this deal, and so they all made their best efforts to figure out how they could manage a business they knew nothing about. We all believed this deal would be a slam dunk because we had so many smart people with so much expertise to deal with any problems that might arise.

On the Friday night before we were to make our final bid to the bankruptcy court, the CEO pulled me aside and said to me (for about the hundredth time), "Mark, our future is going to be on the line with this acquisition. We're investing a lot of money, so you need to be *100 percent certain* that we can be successful if we acquire this company." I was confident because of all the due diligence and research we had done, and so I reassured him: "Don't worry about it. We've done a lot of work, and I know what we need to do to run these companies."

Meanwhile, our due diligence team had arranged for me to meet with one final person who had considerable knowledge of Crystal Brands, as he was one of its former presidents who had run Monet. We hadn't been able to connect until the Friday before the deal was to be finalized on Monday, and we agreed to meet in our offices that evening. He was an older man, and he was very sharp and very direct. As soon as he sat down, he asked me, "What do you know about the women's business?" I said, "Very little." He raised an eyebrow and asked again, "Your company has no women's experience?" and I said, "No. That's not really our business. We're a men's fashion business." He was surprised, and he asked me somewhat incredulously, "Then how can you take on a jewelry business?" He went on to say, "The jewelry business is foreign even to people who work in women's fashions, and it's even more foreign than women's fashions is to men's! There are so many nuances to the women's jewelry business. You really have to be careful, and I don't really understand what you're doing even *considering* acquiring this business. I think you're barking up the wrong tree. I think you're making a mistake."

How's that for direct?

As he continued to talk, he made me more and more uncomfortable. Then, at one point in our conversation, I opened up the subject of surplus inventory. This is a big issue in any business because very often the product you *don't* make can save you a lot of money. If you have inventory problems—in this case too much inventory because you manufactured too much—you have to discount, and that eats away at your margins. In addition, you ruin the equity of the brand. Not managing inventory problems can kill a business.

As we started to discuss this, we either hadn't asked the question properly or something we were talking about made me think of it, and so I asked him, "By the way, what do you do with your surplus?" He said, "We sell some to the off-price channel but most of it we grind up." That shook me, so I asked, "What do you mean you grind it up?" He said, "It's not worth selling. We can't get our money out of it, so it's easier to grind it up." When I heard that, I was really concerned, because in the entire history of my career and all the businesses we have been in, the concept of destroying inventory had never come up, and it showed me that we were dealing with something so different from our areas of experience that we might as well have been dealing with aliens. I felt like I was on Mars. Some brands destroy surplus inventory to protect the integrity of a brand, but destroying it because it is *worthless* is scary!

As soon as our conversation was over, I called the CEO at home. In spite of all the work we had done, I was no longer confident that I could deliver successfully. This was Friday night, and it was late when I called him, but as soon as I told him I was neither comfortable nor confident, we agreed right then and there that on Monday we would not make an offer for the entirety of the Crystal Brands Company. He probably wasn't comfortable either. We decided to walk away from the Monet business, although we would negotiate for Gant and Izod only, which we eventually bought. We outbid management's offer with an all-cash deal.

My point here is that there are a lot of deals you can make and there are a lot of good opportunities that may come your way, but sometimes saying no is more important than saying yes. Sometimes the best deal is the one you walk away from. We had almost talked ourselves into it, but fortunately, at the eleventh hour, we realized this wasn't the business for us to be in. Rather than risk the company, we walked away. That was the right decision for us, and it may be the right decision for you some day. Don't let your desire to do a deal (for whatever reason) influence your decision. Take the emotion out of your decision and focus on the cold, hard facts. If they indicate that the deal should work, by all means go forward. But if you have any hesitation at all, don't be afraid to walk away.

> Sometimes the best deal is the one you walk away from.

19

Who's That Weirdo?

Although we didn't buy Monet from Crystal Brands, we did buy its Izod brand, and I was chosen to manage and integrate the brand into the company. For 25 or 30 years, the Izod brand was recognizable by the alligator logo that it shared with a French company (Lacoste) that had licensed it to Izod. The two brands were intertwined and were called Izod/Lacoste.* By the time we bought Izod, its previous owner had sold the alligator mark back to the French company to try to avoid bankruptcy, and so the alligator is now strictly a Lacoste symbol.

Anyway, we bought Izod after it went bankrupt (as mentioned in Chapter 18; we bought Gant as well), because we thought it was a very powerful brand that still had enormous potential. We believed we could turn it into something very exciting. Izod was my true passion. I had loved the Van Heusen brand, but Izod replaced that love and passion. Purchasing this brand marked the first time PVH had risked it all, and the CEO and the board were counting on me to make it work. I had never taken anything so personally. I can tell you, in the first year after we bought the company, we canceled more orders than we shipped. But in our first full year, we outsold all our projections, and we were on a roll. That was one of the happiest periods in my career.

Izod was a very powerful brand in the golf world, which was very different from any of the other businesses with which we were familiar. At the time, I didn't know much about golf. (When you grow up in

---

*In fact, it's one of the great marketing blunders of all time that this French company allowed its name to be associated with Izod on the same label. That's a Harvard case study for another time.

Brooklyn, you don't play golf.) However, as vice chair of the company with responsibility for all our sportswear brands, I needed to learn about golf.

The first thing I learned was that most of the golf wear at that time in the United States was sold through pro shops in country clubs. I went to my first sales trade show with the president of the Izod division, who reported to me. Izod was competing at that time with three huge mega sports brands. We needed to find a way to compete; that was really difficult, but we were working on it.

At the golf trade show, however, the Izod brand was huge. We had one of the biggest trade booths in the entire show, with 32 salespeople working it. We had premier positioning because we were one of the major factors in the golf industry. I remember thinking how difficult it was for our other product lines to penetrate department stores. We weren't small here: we were one of the kings in this business. It was just amazing.

As I walked around the trade show, I noticed that all the golfers and all the salespeople looked like military guys: they were buff, with short-cropped hair. They looked like serious athletes, not businessmen. Many, it turns out, had hopes of being professional golfers, but clearly, they all had the look. Suddenly, the president pointed to the entrance of our booth and said, "Get a look at *that* guy: What's *he* doing here?" I turned and saw this freaky-looking guy with long, straight black hair, and right away I recognized Alice Cooper. He looked out of place, but I was intrigued, and so I walked over to him and the man he was with and said, "Hello. I'm Mark Weber. What can I do for you guys?"

I soon learned that Alice is serious about golf: he will tell you he gave up all his addictions for golf. I found out later that he's also a great golfer: he tries to play every day, and he's excellent at it; I know, I played with him. Even when he went on tour, he played golf. He told me he was at this trade show because he was looking for a sponsor for his charitable foundation, Solid Rock, which holds an annual celebrity golf tournament to raise money. He started the charity because he believed that if you took high school kids at 3 p.m. and gave them a place for recreation, they would stay out of trouble and off the streets and they would have better lives because they would have something meaningful to keep them busy. That was Solid Rock, an organization and place for teenagers to go and be productive after school.

Alice was looking for a title sponsor. Solid Rock needed a company to outfit about 100 workers and provide gift bags that they could give to the celebrities who were playing in the golf tournament as a thank-you for participating. As soon as Alice said, "We're looking for a sponsor," I said, "Okay, we'll do it." He said, "No, you don't understand. This is a lot of work." I said, "That's okay; consider it done." At this, Alice's foundation manager looked at me and said, "Who are you?" I said, "I'm the president of the company." Silence. The manager looked at me again in disbelief and asked, "You're really going to do this?" And I said again, "It's done. I'll bring over the people. Let's get this thing started. When is your tournament going to be?" From that very moment, I had a deal with Alice Cooper.

I knew I wanted to do this deal because I agreed with their goals and because Alice Cooper was the complete opposite of what you would expect from a golfer. I knew I wouldn't be able to compete directly with the companies that dominated the golf apparel industry (Nike, Adidas), and so I had to find a way to differentiate and appeal to a young market that would want to buy cool, traditional golf apparel. Even Alice Cooper wears golf shirts when he golfs, and so he was my celebrity link to a completely different market.

For the next nine years our company sponsored Alice Cooper's golf tournament. It was a great way to market our brand in the golf industry. Other apparel companies paid pro golfers to wear their hats; for example, at that time companies such as Nike and other big sportswear and equipment manufacturers would pay $250,000 to $500,000 just for a logo on a hat. Pro golfers also "rented out" all the parts of their shirts: they had logos on the right chest, left chest, right sleeve, left sleeve, back, and even on the back of their pants. Each one of those logos was paid for by a major manufacturer or brand marketer. That's sports marketing and an important component of the golf sports marketing industry.

I knew we couldn't compete on that level, and I wasn't convinced it would sell apparel anyway (equipment yes, but not apparel), so I decided we should use celebrity golf tournaments to market and create interest in the Izod brand. My plan would be to make beautiful golf apparel with large Izod logos on the chest or the back neck or the sleeve. We would give these beautiful shirts, pants, windbreakers, and sweaters to the celebrities, and when they went home to their own courses— Riviera Country Club, Bel-Air Country Club, Pebble Beach—they would wear our apparel. That was my strategy—an unconventional way to get our name associated with the finest celebrities in the world.

Alice Cooper had a lot of celebrity friends who golfed, and they came to his tournament.

After that, I went on a tear. It felt right, it was cost-effective, we were involved with the movie and music industry, and we were helping people. I thought we could establish our brand with influencers.

I started looking around for other celebrity charity tournaments that we could sponsor. I contacted Shep Gordon, whom I had met and who is Alice Cooper's longtime manager. Shep introduced me to Michael Douglas, who always had the crème de la crème of celebrities at his tournaments. Every year, he invited 16 friends to play; one year, he had Sylvester Stallone, James Woods, Clint Eastwood, James Garner, Jerry Weintraub, and many other world-class celebrities.

After that we sponsored the American Film Institute's golf tournament, where I met Mark Wahlberg, and we played together and eventually became pretty good golf friends. We even sponsored Mark's charity event in Boston. Another year Jack Nicholson played at that tournament, and that led to our sponsoring Jack's own tournament, where Adam Sandler played with us, among others. Thus, these sponsorships built on one another, and we've continued to use them as a marketing vehicle to put our shirts and clothes literally on the backs of various very well-known celebrities.

It was a bit of a gamble that the celebrities would wear the shirts. If they did, though, they would be seen by even wider audiences, because many these tournaments except for Alice Cooper's were televised. That added to the promotional value of giving free hats or shirts to the celebrities: if they wore them and were seen on TV, that would enhance the Izod brand, too.

At one tournament we had thousands of hats made for the celebrities to wear. Of course, we couldn't guarantee that they would wear them, but most of them accepted that it was a courtesy to do so. I had access everywhere because by that time I had been doing this for years. A few other people and I waited outside the locker room where all the celebrities exited to go onto the golf course, and we handed out hats: whatever color the person was wearing, we gave him a hat in a matching color.

Joe Pesci was playing in this tournament, and when he exited the locker room, I said, "Hello, Mr. Pesci. I have a great hat to match your outfit." He looked at me and said, "F*&^ you. Get out of my face." And he swatted my hand away. Remember, I wasn't the cleaning crew (not that they should be treated that way either). I was the president of the company, but I guess he didn't know that or didn't care. Actually, I thought it was hysterical.

It so happened that the tournament director was there when this happened. It's a privilege for these celebrities to be invited to these tournaments, because the sponsors are very generous and it was a beautiful resort. Of course, the tournament organizers also want the celebrities to come, but when the tournament director saw how Joe Pesci responded to me, he said, "I promise you, Mark, when that TV camera starts rolling, he'll be wearing your hat." And he was: I have a picture to prove it.

This type of promotion has proved to be a pretty clever approach to marketing, and it has paid off. Moreover, it hasn't really cost us much at all, and it has increased business awareness of our products. Best of all, the Izod brand became well known among music and film stars in Hollywood.

20

We Liked
Everything We
Saw but Nothing
We Heard

B y 2003 the PVH company was a great company: it was professionally managed, well organized, and very well thought out. It ran like a bank. All the senior managers were very smart. We managed our inventory extremely well. We always made significant profits while maintaining a sense of fairness not only toward the people who worked for us but around the world as well.

However, we weren't growing. Our assets weren't stagnant, but they were definitely mature: we had a little growth but really no growth engine. We had plateaued, and we were growing only incrementally—about 2 to 5 percent a year. Because we were a public company, that wasn't enough growth to satisfy our shareholders. The stock was languishing. We needed to raise the value of the company. At this point, I was president of PVH and a board member, and so this situation was one in which I was deeply vested.

It became clear that we needed a *transforming transaction*: something that would not merely change but transform the company. We started to look for opportunities, and we found several companies that we thought might be great for us to acquire.

We looked at a growing island lifestyle brand very closely, but we were concerned that it didn't have enough product lines for year-round sales, and so we walked away from it and it was eventually bought by another company. We looked at another company that had a very big apparel conglomerate, about $2 billion in annual sales, but as we got close to buying it, I pointed out to the CEO that there wasn't a single name in its portfolio that we could put over the door of a retail store because nobody really knew any of its brands, plus it needed fixing. We had spent a number of years fixing our company, so why open ourselves up to someone else's headaches? We walked away from that deal, too.

Then we talked about acquiring Warnaco, which had gone into bankruptcy. Warnaco was the largest licensee of Calvin Klein (which was a publicly held company in bankruptcy), and it was being run by a turnaround company, Alvarez & Marsal, that had positioned it for sale. Warnaco's product lines included Calvin Klein underwear, Calvin Klein jeans, Speedo, and several other brands that weren't of interest to us (and I've therefore forgotten). We were really interested only in the jewel of Warnaco's collection, which was the Calvin Klein business.

Earlier, I talked about how sometimes the best deal is the one you walk away from, and that proved to be true here, too. As we started doing our due diligence and looking hard at Warnaco, we liked everything we saw but nothing we heard. After all, something had put them into bankruptcy. We met with the managers of each division and asked all the relevant questions: Where are you in terms of market share? What's doing well? What's not doing well? What does your distribution look like? Are you important to your stores? How much volume do you do? The answers to all these questions were good, very good; we were feeling positive. The thrill of the hunt.

However, we found a red flag when we asked, What is it like working with the Calvin Klein Company? This was very important because the CK Company was the owner of the brand and had creative control over everything. Every time we asked this question, we got the same answer: they told us how difficult it was to deal with what they called "those fanatics." Apparently, the CK people were very protective of their brand, and the Warnaco people told us that the Warnaco designs were controlled by the CK people: "If we said we need black turtlenecks, for example, they told us, 'Well, we believe in purple.' And we got purple, not the black that we knew we could sell." I'll never forget them telling us that.

As we met with each and every division, it became clear to us that Calvin Klein and the CK Company managed their image and the positioning of their brands so tightly that if we bought the Warnaco company, we would be putting our own franchise and business at risk. Although we respected the discipline of the brand and admired the "fanaticism," we knew we couldn't allow someone to have that kind of control over us, particularly in a transaction of this size and scope.

While we were mulling what to do, someone—I don't recall who, but I think it was Peter Solomon, who was on our board—suggested that we buy Calvin Klein itself rather than Warnaco, following the old adage "Why buy the cow if you can get the milk for free?" In other words, why buy Warnaco out of bankruptcy if it was going to be so difficult dealing with Calvin Klein as a licensor? Why not buy Calvin Klein instead and have control over everything? It became very clear to us very quickly that this was an extremely exciting idea. Bruce decided we were going to go after Calvin, and he made it happen.

(I should mention that Peter Solomon welcomed me very warmly when I was made president of the company. We had a board meeting on the day it was announced to the company and the industry: when I walked into the meeting to present, as I would normally do, everyone was clapping, and there was an empty seat at the table. That was when they told me that I had also been given a seat on the board. On one side of me was Bruce, and on the other was Peter Solomon, and they both shook my hand and said, "Mr. President, you're now a member of the board.")

The Calvin Klein Company was privately held by Calvin Klein and his partner, Barry Schwartz. The company was divided primarily into two components: certain businesses that they ran themselves and a tremendous business that was licensed out to other companies. It was a royalty machine; for example, Warnaco had the license for Calvin Klein underwear and sold about $400 million worth annually (at that time) of that product line alone, for which CK received royalties. Warnaco sold another $500 million annually in Calvin Klein jeans around the world, for which CK also received royalties. In addition, CK licensed its name to Unilever for fragrances (Eternity, Obsession, and others), and CK collected royalties on those products, too. In total, the Calvin Klein company collected a very large royalty stream—announced at that time as $100 million a year—with a large infrastructure to manage, design, and control most of its licensees. If we bought the company, *we* would control them.

The Calvin Klein Company wasn't officially for sale until we approached them with an offer to buy. Fortunately, at least one of the partners was interested in selling the company. Then several other companies became interested, and we got involved in a bidding war. We won, and we took over the Calvin Klein Company.

During the bidding war and negotiations, which took about three months, Bruce Klatsky and the CFO, Manny Chirico, focused on acquiring the funds to buy Calvin Klein. Meanwhile I, as the president and COO, focused on studying how the company ran, with the idea that when we took over, we would know all the businesses of Calvin Klein Inc. We would be prepared to develop new businesses and would know which businesses to license and which businesses or functions were to be changed or eliminated—in short, we were determining an operating strategy and vision should we be successful in acquiring the company. We knew the brand was strong. We knew it was run as a private company with a different expense structure (which a private company is entitled to do), but as a public company, we realized we had to streamline a lot of the operations, take out a lot of the costs, and focus the business on building and growing. That's what we did, and it was a huge success

This deal wouldn't have had a happy ending if we had bought Warnaco, as we originally intended, even though it would have been a transformational opportunity for the company. However, the risk associated with dealing with Calvin Klein's apparent ironclad control was too great for us to take on. That risk was a critical component of our decision and one you need to keep in mind when you're considering opportunities in your job or business. You have to be prepared to say no regardless of how enticing something is. No matter how attractive a deal is, there are times that you need to walk away, and when you look back later in life, it could be one of the best decisions you ever made.

We now owned the Calvin Klein brand. And by the way, for those folks from PVH who never heard of me after the sandblasting, I was the president of PVH and the chief operating officer. In addition to overseeing all of their businesses and brands, I had the operational responsibility for Calvin Klein. And the Calvin Klein CEO, Tom Murry, a very capable executive and a good guy, reported to me. We both learned from each other and built this brand.

A little later on my life at PVH was to change. But I will never forget, after being at Calvin Klein for about a year, after the board applauded our efforts, my management teammates were up at Calvin with Tom and I and we watched them try to make phone calls. They couldn't. To dial out at Calvin you had to start with 8, not 9 as in PVH. Just goes to show you who did the work!

21

My Friend Gene

Knowing when to walk away from a deal is important, but being open to new opportunities and new contacts is also important. I mentioned in Chapter 19 that after the company bought Izod, I became interested in the golf world and started playing regularly. It's not a cliché that a lot of business is conducted on the golf course: you have the opportunity to meet new people and get to know them pretty well as you're walking an 18-hole course. And sometimes those people become friends—and business partners.

I started playing golf at public courses, but after a couple of years I grew tired of the difficulty of getting a tee time, and so I finally decided to join a private golf club. The first time I went to Seawave Country Club, I was putting on my golf shoes and feeling a bit uncomfortable because I didn't know anyone, whereas everyone around me was in a foursome or with a partner. Then this elder statesman came over to me and said, "I know you. You're Mark Weber. I'm Gene Rothkopf." I smiled and said hello and asked how he knew me. He said, "Of course I know you: I work in the apparel industry. I have my own consulting firm. I've followed your career. You and I should play golf one day." I told him I would love to—and I meant it.

I was really pleased that he came over and introduced himself. First of all, I always had instant respect for anyone whose hair was grayer than mine, because I was raised to respect my elders. Second, he was the only person who made an effort to say hello to me, and he certainly didn't need to reach out to me: I found out later that he had been a member of the club for 25 years and knew just about everyone there. We made a date to play golf the next week.

As we played that day, we naturally started to talk, and I found out that his practice specialized in licensing and other financial transactions, including mergers and acquisitions. He told me he knew my company had bought Calvin Klein, and he said, "Let me know if I can do anything." I told him I had a couple of deals in the works, but I would certainly keep him in mind in the future.

Over the next few months, Gene and I talked about various deals and ideas, but because Calvin Klein had a big licensing network, I didn't need him to help. Instead, I asked him to find opportunities in areas of the business that either I personally or my company as a whole was unfamiliar with. One of the people he introduced me to was Sammy Aaron, who ran a privately held outerwear business, including a license for St. John's. Gene asked if I would be interested in meeting Sammy to discuss a possible outerwear license with Calvin Klein. We already had a license for outerwear; nonetheless, I agreed to meet Sammy. When I did, I immediately liked him: he's a great guy, and I felt he had what it takes to be successful in this business. At the time, however, I couldn't do business with him because our needs didn't overlap.

About a month later, though, the company that had the license for Calvin Klein outerwear was in trouble and about to go bankrupt. I went to meet with the owner, who confirmed he was having financial problems. I wanted him to forfeit the Calvin Klein license; he refused. He believed his company could recover from its financial difficulties and still have a future. As much as I would have liked to help him, I was familiar with bankruptcy law and the issues: if your brand gets caught in bankruptcy procedures, the licensee stays with the bankrupt company. In other words, our Calvin Klein outerwear license would be tied up in court, and the judge might very well say, "We want to give this company a chance, and to do so, we can't separate this license because it's not fair to the shareholders and the lenders. Having this license may be the only way the company can get back on its feet."

Although that would be good for the licensee, it wouldn't be at all good for my company. I was nervous that this license could get caught up in bankruptcy for who knew how long, so I called Gene immediately and said, "I want you to call Sammy Aaron and see if he's still interested in licensing outerwear with us. I want $1 million on signing. I want $1 million guaranteed per year. I'm willing to sign a five-year license, but I need to know within an hour whether or not he'll do it. And one more kicker: I need him to hire the president of the company who owns the license: he wants to work!"

Forty minutes later, Gene and Sammy Aaron were on the phone: "We'll give you a $1 million sign-on bonus. We'll take over the license.

We'll hire the guy on a temporary basis to see if it works out." With that, we did the deal.

Today, Gene and his partners at Jassin Consulting represent close to $1 billion worth of retail sales of products licensed for CK that we began together since our first game on the golf course; Gene has put together deals for Donna Karan International as well. Yet this very successful business relationship would never have happened if Gene hadn't introduced himself to me that day at the golf club. (Sammy Aaron eventually needed our approval to sell his company with CK license to a growing conglomerate, GIII, which I granted, and that led to many other Calvin Klein licensing deals.) My point is that you never know who you're saying hello to or who you're going to meet either directly or through others, as I met Sammy through Gene. Put yourself out there and be happy to meet anyone who wants to introduce himself to you. Shake hands and be friendly, because you never know where that handshake can lead. Gene really understood how to win friends and influence people: he made a conscious decision to be friendly to me when he didn't have to. He also knew I was in his field and had an important job, and in this case he extended an invitation to play golf that turned into $1 billion worth of opportunity simply because he decided to befriend me.

Interestingly, as I got to know Gene over the years, I learned he did things like that all the time. He's someone whom everyone likes—maybe because he seems like an elder statesman, or because he's noncontroversial, or because he knows how to talk to people and make people feel important. He knows how to make deals. When Gene calls, people answer.

I'm sure that some of you reading this story may be skeptical or cynical and think, I introduce myself and meet new people every day, I give my card out regularly, and I even give free advice to help people I meet, yet I've never had it pay off for me. That certainly happens: I could write a book about people who have underwhelmed me or haven't handled situations the way I think they should have. There are a lot of jerks out there, and human nature never ceases to disappoint me. In this case, however, I'm describing someone who did something smart. When Gene sat down next to me in that golf cart, I didn't think anything other than that I had made a new friend. But he found a way to talk to me without being pushy, offering to help, telling me about his company and how it worked, saying that no assignment was too difficult. And just a few months later, he proved that.

> I know how hard it is out there. I know what it's like to be without a job, and I believe that if you can help someone else, that's the best way you can spend your time.

My friend Ken Wise, who is president of licensing at PVH, has said to me, "Anyone who is successful is always willing to help others. And the more senior they are, the more willing they are to help." That's the way I've always led my life. If somebody comes to me and asks for help, I'm ready and willing to do whatever I can. I know how hard it is out there. I know what it's like to be without a job, and I believe that if you can help someone else, that's the best way you can spend your time.

I'm glad I've always lived my life that way, because little did I know how soon I would be reaching out to others and asking for help.

22

The Termination

A few years before PVH bought the Calvin Klein Company, Bruce Klatsky started to talk about retiring. He had fulfilled the goal he told me about on my first day at PVH, and I had followed him to become president (I would eventually become CEO, too). Every time he brought up retiring, however, I didn't believe him. We had a great management team in place, and we were doing exceptionally well. He was only in his late fifties, and so it seemed too early for him to retire. Then, after we purchased Calvin Klein, PVH was flying. We knew we were on a great roll: we had done what we needed to do to make Calvin Klein work, the company's stock started to appreciate, and the future of the company looked terrific. Bruce again brought up the subject of retiring.

I had been president of the corporation for about six or seven years, and I was a member of the board; I was the number two guy in the company. Because Bruce and I had worked well together for more than 30 years, if he retired, I didn't feel very secure that my future would be what I wanted it to be. If the company brought in a new CEO, that CEO might bring in another person above me, or replace me. I felt that I had earned clarity. And if the company didn't make me CEO, I knew I would want to leave. I shared my concerns with Bruce, and he said something that I thought was interesting but silly: "If I retire and the company chooses not to make you the CEO, all you need to do is behave improperly, the board will fire you, and you'll get your severance." I told him, "That makes no sense: I have 30 years invested, and the company and I deserve better!"

I thought that was an inappropriate way to look at my future with the company, and I told him so. I also told him how much I had enjoyed working with him all these years and that if the board didn't want me to become CEO after he retired, I would prefer to leave at the same time.

I thought this was fair, it protected me, and I assured the company the number two guy would stay.

Bruce met with the compensation committee and negotiated with them on my behalf: if he retired as CEO and I was not named the new CEO, I would walk off with what I called a sunset contract (Bruce and I would "walk off into the sunset" together). The board agreed and rewrote my agreement. The board was generous and appreciative of my position, and I really appreciated that. It lessened my concerns for the future, although I truly believed Bruce would never retire and the board would never make me CEO.

There were a number of people on the board who liked me and recognized my contributions, but I knew some of the board members did not. I was a different type of person from Bruce: I was more interested in the product and the marketing, and although I demonstrated substance and corporate durability, they just didn't see past my exterior. I believe I became the youngest division president in the history of the company because nobody took me seriously, and so they didn't see me as a competitor. In fact, I was told once that whereas others in the company were "killing each other off" in their political clamber up the career ladder, I just kept moving up because everyone underestimated me. All they saw was my style, not the substance. Yet character wins. I was a really serious guy who had some talent and who was learning everything I could as fast as I possibly could.

Not long afterward, it became clear that the Calvin Klein acquisition was doing very well and our CEO decided to retire, and he told me he believed the board would appoint me as the next CEO. However, when I met with the member of the board who was the lead person on the nomination committee, I was told that the board wanted to interview me about becoming CEO. I found that surprising, and I told them so: "I've been here 30 years. You guys know who I am. However, if you're going to run a beauty contest and go outside and start looking around and talking to other people, then I'd just like to leave. I'm more than willing to simply take my sunset contract. I'd like to be CEO. If you want me to stay, then I need to be your candidate for CEO."

The board restated its interest in me but also let me know that the Sarbanes-Oxley regulations (which were new and ongoing at that time) required boards everywhere to have greater oversight, particularly in a CEO transition. Therefore, our board members wanted to make sure they did everything properly if they were going to appoint an internal candidate to become the next CEO. When I accepted the interview process as part of complying with the new regulations, I said, "Okay; I'll follow any process you want to go through to ensure that you are comfortable with your decision. I'm ready to go."

I found the interviews very disturbing: most of the questions the board members asked me were things they should have known; after all, I had worked more than 30 years at the company, and I had been both president and a board member for 7 years. Yet they didn't know enough about my background. They asked me what jobs I had had and how I had gotten to where I was. I have the highest regard for every-one on that board, and I don't think they were doing anything wrong, and they were certainly entitled to have the CEO they preferred. The board had a solemn obligation to act with great diligence in naming the CEO: I respected that and the process. I have no hard feelings about any of this. Still, I thought it was odd that they didn't know more about my background, since this was the only company I had ever worked at and I had been so visible for so long.

Then the compensation committee got involved in negotiating my financial package. Right up front, I told them I understood that the former CEO had been CEO for 11 years, and as a new CEO, I didn't expect to have the same compensation package he had. I told them I wanted to be fair and I was sure that they did, too.

But as the negotiations dragged on, the situation became increas-ingly uncomfortable for me. I had a very good compensation attorney, Stewart Reifler of Vedder Price, who said, "Mark, something doesn't feel right here. I've never seen an incoming CEO being treated in a negotiation the way they're treating you. When a company goes out-side to find a CEO, the conversations can be complicated, because the board really doesn't know that person; they do their best to vet the candidates, but even when they make a decision, they don't really know what they're getting. But you've been with this company for a long time, you've made contributions, and you earned your way—yet the way they're negotiating with you just doesn't feel like they're applauding and getting excited about you coming in. This just doesn't feel right to me." I thought about what he said, which seemed to be the first signal from an objective insider that something was a little off.

The negotiations continued until finally I said to the lead director of the compensation committee, "This is not going anywhere. I don't want to discuss my compensation any longer. I'll accept whatever you give me as long as you can sleep at night. I'm through negotiating about money. But I will not sign a noncompete, and I want my severance package to be more of a safety net than the current package I have in my sunset contract. That's all I ask for." The negotiation ended with that compromise.

This entire process had begun in October 2004, and by November or December it was decided that I would become the next CEO. The board elected me, and the company and the press were notified that the official handover would be made at our June 2005 annual shareholders meeting. Until then, I would spend the time assuming the role and working with the outgoing CEO: in effect, I was acting CEO from the beginning of 2005.

Fast-forward to the night before the annual meeting in June. We arranged a going-away party for Bruce. We invited the board members and every officer of the company and all their spouses or significant others: about 200 people. We oversaw an extensive preparation and program, including key speakers, awards, and a global video that reached out to all our foreign offices and many of Bruce's family members and corporate friends. The preparations were extensive.

There were three of us who were planning and setting up this meeting: Henry Justus, the head of marketing; Manny Chirico, the CFO; and me. I was very close with many people in the company, but I was particularly close to Henry, who was a great friend and a great marketing collaborator. About two weeks before the party, I asked Henry, "Has anybody said anything to you about how they plan to announce me taking over as CEO? Is anyone planning to give a toast that night, anything?" When he said he hadn't heard anything, I asked him to do me a favor. I said, "No matter what happens, unless someone comes to you and says, 'The CEO is leaving, and we should think about doing something for the new CEO,' I don't want you to suggest that to anyone. I need your word." He agreed.

Sure enough, on the night of the party the focus was completely on the exiting CEO. There was no toast offered, and no one said anything to me about becoming CEO other than Bruce saying how happy and comfortable he was in "turning over the reins" to me. Even though I wasn't surprised, it was still quite telling. He was leaving, and with all due respect, it seemed there should be some focus on the future. It was another signal that something was off, although I didn't say a word.

The next day was our annual shareholders meeting, and after we had discussed all the information that we always provide, Bruce got up to say a few final words. He gave a very heartfelt speech about his time with the company, what he hoped he had accomplished, how proud he was of the company, and how pleased he was that Mark Weber, his long-term partner with such a strong track record, would succeed him.

Then he turned the podium over to me. I am a pretty good public speaker—over the years, I've worked hard to learn how to present well, which was especially challenging for me given how I started out in life. That day I was especially well prepared, and I gave what I thought was one of the best speeches I had ever given. At the end of my speech, all the board members simply got up and left to go to our board meeting. None of them said anything to me personally or even shook my hand. I managed to corner one and bring him over to meet my wife. But I felt their reaction to me—or the lack thereof—was peculiar. It seemed they were almost avoiding talking to me directly. There was no camaraderie.

After that meeting, I simply went to work in my new position. By the beginning of the next year, however, the board and I were having issues; we just didn't agree. I had been told to spend a lot of time with the board, to seek their counsel, because we were a public company and that was the way it was done. Yet the company was prospering, we were taking our earnings up, and I thought I was doing great. So I didn't spend time with the board, and I can't comment really on their reasons for not wanting me to remain with the company. Maybe I was partly at fault because I didn't present the way they wanted to be presented to. Maybe they didn't want me because the previous CEO had been such a dominant figure and so in command that they simply hadn't ever paid attention to his number two. Maybe we didn't connect because the number three guy was a financial guy and that was what the board members gravitated to more than to me, since I came from the merchant side of the business.

Whatever the reason, in February 2006 I was called in and told that I would no longer be the CEO, that they appreciated everything I had done for the company, and that I would be receiving everything I was entitled to in my contract. They were more than fair to me. I knew I had never been their choice for CEO, but even though I wasn't surprised this had happened, I certainly wasn't happy. Moreover, the meeting I had with them was off-site, so I never even went back to the company. That was it: my long tenure was over.

I've never talked about this publicly, the board has never talked about it, and my successors at PVH have never talked about it (at least to my knowledge). Interestingly, on the day I was let go, PVH took its earnings up for the year to assure Wall Street that there were no problems with the business. What I've just described is supposition, since I obviously can't talk with any authority about the decisions that the board of directors made. I can only surmise. I know that the number one role of a board is to elect its CEO. Even so many years later, I respect the board's courageous actions, and I applaud their well-executed plan.

After the board let me go, I had the unenviable task of telling my wife that I had lost my job. I called her and said, "I need to meet you. It's important." She was surprised; I don't think I had ever called and asked her to meet me during a workday, but she came. We met in a restaurant, and as soon as we sat down, I said, "I have some bad news to tell you." She looked worried. "I was fired today." She hesitated a moment, collected herself, then punched me in the arm and said, "Don't ever scare me like that again. I thought it was something important." My wife is great that way: she always puts life in perspective. She has always been very well grounded.

> Celebrate your successes and recognize that they took your job but they can't take away your skills. There is a new and exciting opportunity out there if you plan properly.

Then she said, "Why are you surprised? Don't you remember what happened at the annual meeting or at the tribute dinner? He was leaving, and you were the new CEO, yet no one thanked you for all you had done or congratulated you on your new position. No one even gave you a toast. Then you forgot what I told you after the board meeting. While you were giving your speech, all the board members were looking down, taking notes, doing anything to avoid looking at you. Nobody seemed to be all that happy. Even worse, when you came down from the stage, not a single board member came over to wish you luck or to meet me and talk with us about your future." So it wasn't a surprise to her—or, I guess, to me.

Fortunately, I didn't have a noncompete: that was one of the points I had insisted on when I negotiated my original deal. Still, I now had to figure out what to do next. I had never been in this position before. I had never lost a job. I had never been fired. I had been demoted, but

I'd always fought back. Here there was no reprieve. I hadn't looked for a job in more than 30 years. I had been working steadily since I was 15 years old, and I had no clear idea what lay ahead for me. I was comfortable financially, but I was career-lost.

At a time like this, the most important thing you can do for yourself is to take a moment to count your blessings. Celebrate your successes and recognize that they took your job but they can't take away your skills. There is a new and exciting opportunity out there if you plan properly. That's exactly what I did.

The Search

23

It's Not How Far You Fall; It's How High You Bounce Back

General George Patton said, "The test of success is not what you do when you are on top. Success is how high you bounce back when you hit the bottom." I thought a lot about that quote after I was fired from the company for which I had worked for more than 30 years.

Although it wasn't a surprise to me that I was let go, I was told later that everyone else in the company was shocked. I had been an institution in that company. Everybody knew I had worked my way up from clerk to president and then CEO and also knew I had always had a terrific track record. Moreover, the reaction to the news was awkward, to say the least. I learned a lot about the people I knew: the people I expected would be my greatest allies at that point in my life turned out to be the greatest disappointments, and people I never expected to step up turned out to be very special. I was—and still am—very grateful to them; I've never forgotten a single one of them, and with any one of them who needed help since that time, I have tried to be a solid citizen.

That first week after I was let go was brutal. I started calling people I thought I could trust, people I was friendly with in business, people I expected would help. But *no one* wanted to take my calls. I was really disappointed that some of my closest friends in business avoided speaking with me. Many—I would say all but two—sent me e-mails, though. I have cherished those e-mails to this day. The other two I have no use for. Maybe they were embarrassed and didn't know what to say to me. I didn't know what they were thinking; all I knew was that they weren't taking my calls, and that was very unpleasant. An interesting response to a call came from a headhunter who had become somewhat of a friend. He said, "You're radioactive. Disappear for six months." Seriously? I wanted to get on with my life—and my career.

I had devoted a lifetime to that company and had only good memories, and being severed from it really took a toll on me. My life changed in an instant: people used to line up for an appointment to meet with me because I was "an important guy" at a big public company, but now they wouldn't even talk to me. It was very humbling, and I experienced a wide gamut of negative emotions: denial, anger, and disappointment. I remember sitting in my home office alone, thinking about what I should do next, and I actually broke down in tears. Five seconds later I collected myself and thought, This can't stand. I'll figure this out. I had had a great career and was not going to let it end on that note. I wanted to come back and do something of consequence.

By Friday of that first week, the company had filed a statement with the SEC, as required by law, because I was a corporate officer of a public company. That statement made clear that I had been severed from the company but there was *no wrongdoing*, and the terms of the contract would be honored in full. That changed my situation dramatically. It was like someone had stuck a pin in a balloon: suddenly, all the air came out, and there were no more concerns. I was able to get on with my life because it had been stated publicly.

I thought about what to do next. It was March, and the weather started changing, so I took a trip with my wife, Susie, and my younger son, Jesse (my other son, Jarrod, was working). We went to Las Vegas, played golf, and had a great time. I started to think that maybe I would just retire, but I gave that idea only three minutes' thought. Then I said to myself that I had had a stellar career, and just because a few people didn't think I was right for their company, I wasn't going to let that be the exclamation mark at the end of my career. I just decided, That's it. I am not retiring. I'm going to come back and try and be as excited about my next opportunity as I possibly can. From there, I started to plan my future.

It wasn't easy. I had never looked for a job—not since I was just out of college. I had never been fired—publicly fired! I had had a few setbacks in my career and promotions I didn't get right away, but I always came back stronger. Because I had no experience of being out of work, I had no idea how to approach this situation. You might not have a lot of sympathy for an unemployed CEO, but it was no fun regardless of how high I was in the hierarchy. Like you, I'm human.

I started to craft a plan for my career the same way I would craft a strategic plan for a company. First, I made a list of my strengths and my weaknesses for my own assessment only: I'll talk about my strengths all day long, but I'll never talk about my weaknesses publicly to anyone. I don't think people should call out their own deficiencies.

I realize this is a popular question during job interviews: Tell me about your strengths and weaknesses. Some interviewees try to be coy by disguising a strength as a weakness: they might say, "I'm a workaholic: I put in long hours, and I need to watch that," which they think every employer wants to hear. In my case—and this is my advice to others—if somebody asks me that question, I answer, "I'm prepared to talk to you about my strengths. If you want to find my weaknesses, we'll work together and you'll see if you can find them." My weaknesses are my business, no one else's. I'm a positive person, but I'm also a very private person. (I can't believe I've written this book!)

After I made a list of all my strengths and weaknesses, I made a list of all the people I knew and another list of the people I thought *they* might know if I called them to ask for an introduction. Finally, I made a list of all the companies I admired and asked myself whether anyone on my other two lists might know someone at those companies.

Then I started calling. In 30 days, I made more phone calls than I had in 30 years, following a single strategy: nothing was too big to consider, and nothing was too small. I would leave no stone unturned. I would never look back and say that my ego or pride got in the way of making any phone calls.

I called people I would never dream of working for, not in a million years. I called anyone and everyone and asked whether they were looking for a number two person; if so, I would be willing to work with them. I called the CEOs of companies in which I thought that if I could secure the number two position, maybe I could eventually surpass the CEO and be promoted to the top position. I told headhunters I preferred a CEO position but would eagerly pursue a number two spot.

I called every headhunter who had ever called me about leaving PVH. Over the years I had had offers. I had never pursued any of them (except one), because I was happy working where I was and was doing well. But now it was fair game.

I called everyone I could think of, especially the people I thought were the smartest. I called people I admired about jobs I thought might make sense for me. However, I didn't prioritize my list. People have asked me why I didn't make these calls more selectively, for example, by first calling the companies I would most like to work for. If those calls led me nowhere, I could call people at companies the next level down, in other words, companies that I would be willing to work for but that I wasn't wild about. And if those calls led nowhere, I could call people at the next level down: companies I didn't really want to work for but that I would work for rather than not working at all. I didn't prioritize because that didn't even occur to me: I wanted to open a broad range of thinking, and as mentioned earlier, you never know what opportunity is behind which door. I did wonder, Will I ever work again? Will I ever find something else I'll enjoy doing?

Making all these phone calls didn't mean I was going to accept the first thing that came my way (although I was tempted). I was simply very interested in reaching out and seeing what I could learn. I wanted leads. I had been terminated from a company, and that was a blot on my career regardless of the reasons. Many very intelligent and worldly people were telling me that was not the case. Companies make changes. Think about Steve Jobs being fired from Apple. Think about all the baseball managers who are let go from one team and then thrive at other ball clubs. Nonetheless, I was thrown. I had always been in control. I didn't really know what to do, but I was willing to talk to anyone and see anyone. I had a strategy, and I was working it.

Many of my phone calls led to some very productive meetings. Unfortunately, many of those calls and meetings were difficult, to say the least. In one case, I heard about a company that was looking for a CEO—a big, successful company that I thought would be a great fit for me—and I called the former CEO to ask if he would make an introduction for me. He was friendly on the call and agreed to help me connect, yet later I found out he told someone that I had a lot of nerve to think I could replace him.

In another case, I met with the headhunter who was looking for the CEO of that same company that I thought would be a good fit for me. She disagreed, listing all the reasons I wasn't right for the job, and she refused to send me on an interview. To add insult to injury, she took so many phone calls during our meeting that we barely had a chance to talk about the position. I found her behavior unprofessional, but that was part of my new life.

I learned about a few positions I thought I was right for that I wasn't considered for, and that was disappointing. Even worse, some of those companies ultimately hired people who did not do well and even had a deleterious effect on the companies' success. Their failures looking back didn't make me feel better; they made me feel worse because I knew what *I* could have done for those companies. I got some surprising rejections, and I wasn't getting enough good leads.

Then things started to improve. One of the first people I called was John Howard, an investment banker with Bear Stearns at that time (now at Irving Place Capital), whom I had met when I was the CEO of PVH because he had an interest in one of our brands. At the time, he had an investment in 7 For All Mankind, Stuart Weitzman, and New York & Company retail stores. I went to his office, and we discussed his fashion portfolio. His company had bought 50 percent of 7 For All Mankind. The founder was still there, but he wanted to retire and sell his remaining shares and ownership. John was interested in acquiring the rest of the company, but he needed someone to take a look at it and determine whether the company could grow and expand and whether they could work with the founder for a period of time during the transition in leadership. John thought it might be right for me, and he asked if I would consider flying out to Los Angeles to get a read on the situation.

While all these conversations with various companies and headhunters were going on, I also had a very unusual opportunity come my way that I thought might lead my future career in an entirely different direction. I wrote earlier that I had met many celebrities at the various golf tournaments the company held to promote the Izod business. One of those celebrities was Mark Wahlberg. Over time, we had sought each other out to play together at various golf tournaments, and I had become very fond of him. In fact, I felt comfortable enough that about a year earlier, while we were playing golf one day, I said, "Hey, Mark, why don't you put me on *Entourage*? I could play the father of one of the guys. I would really like to be on the show." He was the executive producer, and even though he probably got asked that all the time, he said if I really wanted to do it, he would make it happen. Nothing happened for quite some time.

Then I played with Mark and he asked what happened. I told him no one called. Let's just say the next day I received a call from Sheila

Jaffe, the famous casting director, who invited me to do a screen test. When Mark Wahlberg and I first started talking about my being on the show, I was the president of PVH and my position was fairly under the radar. By the time Sheila called, however, I was CEO of a public company, and I didn't think it was appropriate for me to appear on a TV show. When I talked to our company's head of marketing, he said, "It's just a screen test; you don't have to actually do the part. Go do it," and so I did. A film crew was due in New York, and I tested.

At first, they wanted to cast me as a salesman in a Ducati motorcycle dealership. I had a few lines, it was a fun experience, and I went back to my day job. Then Sheila called again and said the director liked my screen test and wanted me to do the scene in a real episode. I told her I couldn't be seen endorsing a product that wasn't mine. I also asked her to thank Mark Wahlberg and let him know it was enough for me that he had followed through. Meanwhile, I was moving on.

Then I left PVH, and I was talking to John Howard about flying to LA to look at 7 For All Mankind, when Sheila Jaffe called again for *Entourage*. She had a part she thought I would be right for as an attorney representing Jeremy Piven's character (Ari Gold) in his split from his business partner, played by Malcolm McDowell. She asked if I could come to California to film it. Her schedule happened to coincide with a meeting I had already planned with the founder of 7 For All Mankind, and so I said yes.

They sent me the script and discussed wardrobe, call time, and location address. I was an actor in a hit show! I was to join the Screen Actors Guild that week. I flew to California on Sunday, was scheduled to film the *Entourage* scene on Monday, and would meet with the founder of 7 Jeans on Tuesday. I was excited because my life was moving forward in some very interesting ways. I thought maybe there could be a new life for me in California: I could work for an apparel company and also be an actor. After all, stranger things have happened, and it's not impossible for ordinary people to become successful actors.

Unfortunately, that didn't happen for me. Late Sunday night, the production head called about my filming. They had a location problem, and the shoot was rescheduled from Monday to Tuesday. Obviously, I needed to make a decision—either do *Entourage* or meet with the founder of 7 Jeans. I was disappointed I couldn't do both; I would have loved to be on *Entourage* just as a fun experience. But I needed to keep my top priority in mind: I wasn't working, and what I really wanted was a second act in my fashion career, and so I chose 7. To this day, my sons have never let me live down that decision.

The next day, I met with Peter Koral, the founder of 7 Jeans and a great guy, very cool and a successful entrepreneur who had built his business from the ground up. We really hit it off and had a good meeting, discussing the details of the business and its future. He gave me a tour of his factory and his warehouse, and at the end of the day he said, "Listen, I want to sell the company, and we need someone to come out here. I think you would be perfect."

When I got home, I wrote up a report for John Howard, and we met to discuss it. I told him I thought the company was quite worthwhile, that I really admired it—both what it had achieved and what it could become. I thought that it could expand its product offerings beyond jeans (bottoms) and that the company's best days were in front of it. In short, I thought it would be a wise investment.

I was seriously considering signing on to run 7 For All Mankind— although I want to be clear: John and I had not discussed anything in detail yet—when two people suggested I slow down and make sure this was the opportunity I really wanted to pursue. One was my wife, whose opinion I value above all others. She said, "Mark, you should really think about this. You don't have to jump at the first thing that comes along. I know what you're going through is hard, but you ought to think about taking your time." My wife is beautiful: always was and always will be. I thought she too could pursue acting in Hollywood. Tracy and Hepburn, Brad and Angelina, Mark and Susie! That was in the back of my head.

Then a second person weighed in. My wife and I were driving to dinner on a beautiful night, with the top down on our convertible, when my phone rang. It was Jason Binn, the founder of Niche Media, which publishes lifestyle magazines such as *Hamptons, Ocean Drive, Gotham, Los Angeles Confidential,* and *Vegas.** It's a small world, as they say, and I think John Howard's investment bank was one of Jason's partners in Niche Media. Jason was in his early thirties, and I met him when he first started coming into prominence. He had built a successful business, and I thought he was an impressive guy. We have two very different styles, yet we bonded. As soon as I picked up the phone, he

---

*Today, Jason is the founder of DuJour, a powerful new concept in luxury online and print magazines.

said, "I heard you were talking to John Howard, and I want to talk to you before you make any decisions. Mark, you're a bigger-than-life guy: you've accomplished a lot. Don't come back small."

That call really made an impact on me. First of all, I was so touched that Jason was a stand-up guy who called to talk to me directly in spite of my being out of the industry. Second, I was impressed that he thought enough of me to give me advice. As I said earlier, some of the people I least expected to show up on my doorstep and do right by me were the most helpful. I never ever forgot that phone call.

At the same time, I had been thinking that 7 For All Mankind wasn't the right move for me after all. Nothing was finalized; there had only been initial discussions. Also, since I came from a large public corporation that produced multiple brands, if John Howard had said to me, "I'll bring you in here, and you can oversee everything," I would have been more interested and would probably be there now. But working in a monobrand company was not what I really wanted to do even though I thought very highly of Peter Koral and the company he had built. I told John Howard that, and he understood.*

For whatever reason, it finally clicked. I realized I had an enormous amount of experience in all aspects of the fashion business. No matter who I met or interviewed with, no matter what subject they raised, I had the answers to all their questions. I've always told people, "I don't know if I'm smart; that's for others to decide. But I know I'm well trained." I started to believe again that I had something to offer, that I shouldn't think about what had happened at the end of my time at my previous company; instead, I started to think that the best part of my career was in front of me. And I became convinced that I should wait for the right position to come along.

---

* Later, when I received the job at LVMH and Donna Karan and it was announced in the press, the first person I called was John Howard to thank him for his interest in me. What he said, I'll never forget: "Mark, when I read the article, I didn't understand why you would want to get involved with that problem. Then it occurred to me that if you were unsuccessful, no one would be surprised, but if you were successful, what a statement!"

---------- 24 ----------

The Headline
That Changed
My Life

Three months into my search, I was continuing to set up general meetings, interviews, and investment opportunities. I considered purchasing part or all of certain boutique advertising agencies (a passion of mine). I considered hedge funds and designer and branded company opportunities. I planned full days two or three times a week for meetings: when you're looking for your next opportunity, it's important to be organized, and it's very important to have discipline.

I started to see the light at the end of the tunnel; I felt sure that something was going to happen. I met with a very famous designer about an opportunity, and I had an offer to work at a large brand consolidator. I was playing a number of angles, and I was very close to accepting a job offer.

I was sitting alone in my home office one day when I happened to read a very interesting headline in *Women's Wear Daily* online: "Luxury Companies Can't Find CEOs." When I read it, I actually yelled, "That's because you don't know where to f***ing look, you pompous a**holes."*
I started laughing, but I was also intrigued, especially when the article quoted two headhunters and the names of their companies. One was based in Italy, and the other in New York.

I called the headhunter in Italy first† and said, "I just read the *Women's Wear Daily* article that quoted you about luxury companies not being able to find CEOs. My name is Mark Weber. I was the

---

*I don't swear in public, but in the privacy of my own home I say what I want.
† I don't recall her name or her company.

president and CEO of a public company. I'm looking for work, and if you have something, I'd be very interested in talking to you."

She said, "Thank you for calling. It just so happens I'm looking for a CEO for Marc Jacobs." (Life is funny: Marc Jacobs is owned by LVMH.) I told her I was interested in knowing more, and she asked me to tell her about myself, which I did. Then she asked, "What did you earn?" This is a tricky question for anyone looking for work, and the higher you go and the more money you make, the trickier it is. I said, "Forget what I earned. It's not important. I was CEO of a public company. It's not about money for me right now." I was following the advice Jules Pepper had given me 30 years earlier that money didn't matter, although at this point in my life, it didn't matter for a different reason.

She persisted: "I must know what you earned." I continued to try to put her off this subject, and finally she told me the salary and bonus opportunity of the Marc Jacobs job. I said, "That sounds perfect." She asked me again what I had earned, and when I told her, she got very quiet and said, "I don't think this job is for you." There was no way I could persuade her to let me interview for it. Sometimes monetary success can work against you.

This is a situation a lot of people face when they're looking for work: I know this not only from my own experience (this wasn't the only time it happened) but from talking to other people I've mentored over the years and have helped find new jobs. Whether your salary is $50,000, $500,000, or $5 million, if you're not working and you want to continue to work, you'll often encounter headhunters, human resources managers, and hiring managers who won't even consider you for a job that pays less than your previous position. They think you won't be happy with the pay cut—maybe not at first but eventually. Or they think you won't be challenged by the job because it's not as high-level or prestigious as your previous job or it has less responsibility or less staff and you'll get bored.

Sometimes it's even about the job title: I know many people who were president of their former companies who can't get an interview for a senior vice president position at another company because the hiring manager doesn't believe they will ever be satisfied with the lesser job title. Sometimes a president's title is just that: a title. Sometimes it's not what you would consider a president. An example might be a head of sales who is called the president. Thus, titles can be a problem. Often entrepreneurs will not be hired by major public companies because they think an entrepreneur's spirit won't work well in a corporate environment. It's very difficult to overcome these types of problems.

In my case, if I hadn't been a public figure and my previous salary hadn't been published (and reported), I would have downsized my expectation. But I couldn't: I was caught between a rock and a hard place. Even if your salary isn't published, it's often difficult to circumvent this question, because most job ads require you to list your salary requirements or history, and many companies won't consider you if you don't provide this information. They need to look out for their best interests, not yours, and if they think you're not going to thrive in the job and will be looking to leave the day you start, they don't want you to accept it—or even interview for it.

Nevertheless, my advice is to try to convince the company that whatever the salary is, that's fine with you. That approach doesn't always work, as it didn't with this Italian headhunter, but you should still try, as I did. Eventually she said, "I appreciate you calling me, and I will keep you in mind for something else, but this job is not for you." I was disappointed, but I needed to move on.

There are times when the facts work against you. You have to try to convince whoever you're meeting with that what's really important to you is the job itself. Sometimes that will work, and sometimes it won't. There are always going to be factors that work against you that you have to consider when interviewing. And sometimes, no matter how hard you try to overcome them, you just can't.

After I hung up with the Italian headhunter, I called the New York headhunter who had also been quoted in the *Women's Wear Daily* article. Her name is Maxine Martens, of Martens & Heads. Little did I know that she would change my life. To this day I still seek out her counsel. I consider her a friend, an advocate, and a great business partner.

I didn't reach her right away: when I called, I spoke to her assistant, Nicolaus Shuit. I told him about the article I had read and why I wanted to talk to Maxine, and he assured me she would get back to me. Sure enough, an hour or two later she called. (I'm always impressed by people who respond quickly: I've noticed that all the successful people I've ever met in my life are the ones who return phone calls and e-mails within 24 hours.) I started to introduce myself: "Maxine, you don't know me, but if you're looking for CEOs for luxury companies, maybe you're not looking in the right place." She said, "Mark, I do know who you are: I have a two-inch file with your name on it right here on my desk. I've never called you about a job because I thought you were a lifer with your previous company. Let's meet tomorrow if you're free." I said, "Absolutely."

The next day I went to her office and found her to be one of the smartest, most sophisticated women in the world. She runs her own firm and is really connected in the luxury business. After the introductions, the first thing she asked was, "Who needs you?" and I said, "What?" She repeated, "Tell me the companies that need you." I had never been asked that question, and it really made me think. When I first started making my lists of people I wanted to call, I had thought about what companies *I* wanted to work for, companies I admired, companies where I thought I could contribute something. But I hadn't really thought about what companies *needed* my background, experience, and know-how.

Once she asked the question and I finished stuttering, I immediately thought of several companies that needed me—companies that will remain anonymous for obvious reasons: I don't want to embarrass anyone who's doing the best he or she can. Maxine and I had a very candid conversation about what companies I thought I could improve, companies where I would be a good addition to their team. She also asked many interesting questions to read me. One that I admired was "Tell me one great thing that happened to you this month and one disappointing thing that happened this month."

After a very long and fascinating dialogue on my next career move, Maxine said, "I know something that would be great for you, but I don't know if I can get you in," and she started to talk about Donna Karan International: "They've been looking for a CEO. The head of recruiting at LVMH—Moët Hennessy Louis Vuitton—is Edie Steinberg, and she's far along in the search. I'm not sure you can get through at this late date, but let me talk to her, and I'll get back to you."

I was cautiously optimistic: Donna Karan is a great brand, and I had admired it for many years. It was fate: Donna Karan is the only company interview I had had in 30 years; I had been in line for that job (I'll tell that story in a later chapter). At my previous company, we had licensed the DKNY name for shirts, it was an amazing business, and I respected the brand. I also admired their advertising: I thought (at the time and still to this day) that they had the best men's advertising I ever saw. It was always natural, it was filmed in New York City, and it looked like slices of real life, but with style and substance the likes of which I've never seen. In fact, the first campaign I did when I joined LVMH was a re-creation of their campaign that I had first seen when I was not a part of the company. It hangs in my office. But I'm getting ahead of the story.

The next day I got a call from LVMH's corporate offices, asking if I could meet with Edie Steinberg. Of course I said yes, and the next day we met. I told her who I was, what my background was, and what I was looking for since leaving my former company. I told her that my claim to fame was building brands. I told her that my most recent experience was the acquisition of Calvin Klein and that I believed that success had prepared me well for a position at Donna Karan. We had a wonderful conversation, she thanked me for coming, I told her I appreciated her time, and I left.

Later that day Maxine called to tell me she heard it went well. She still wasn't sure that Edie would put me through as a candidate, but she said she'd keep trying. That same evening Maxine called me again and said, "Edie agreed to consider you because you have the Calvin Klein experience and because of your brand-building experience. It just so happens that the managing director of LVMH is coming to New York next week. Would you be available to meet with him on Tuesday?" Again I said, "Absolutely."

LVMH wanted to find a formula for Donna Karan International. DKI had started as a luxury brand and then invented other components of the business (primarily DKNY and DKNY Jeans), which sold at different price points. LVMH needed to find a way to rationalize that and make the components all work together, in unison, without jeopardizing any part of that pyramid. At the top is the Donna Karan Collection, which consists of dresses selling from $3,000 to $10,000. The next level is DKNY, which makes dresses that sell from $350 to $800. The next level down is DKNY Jeans, which might include a jeans dress priced between $125 and $175. How do you put all that together? How do you organize it? How do you make it work? That was the challenge LVMH was facing. I was ready for that challenge because I had the experience and the training.

On Tuesday, I put on my best suit and went to meet Antonio (Toni) Belloni, the managing director of LVMH (the European equivalent of president), in the company's office tower on 57th Street in Manhattan. Mr. Belloni is a great-looking Italian man with salt-and-pepper hair and a commanding presence. I soon found that he was one of the smartest people I'd ever met—if not the smartest. English is his second language, and although he speaks with an accent, his vocabulary was and is better than I can ever hope for.

He had my résumé, of course, and he began by asking me questions about my background and my experience in the business, especially related to the Calvin Klein acquisition. Then he talked about what was going on with Donna Karan International: they had had three CEOs in six years and needed to hire someone who could put the company on the proper course and run it professionally. They needed a leader! As we talked about the business, I was really impressed with him, and I truly enjoyed our conversation. Then he said he would like me to consider joining Donna Karan.

I found out later that his original plan for this trip from Paris to New York was to meet with other candidates whom LVMH was seriously considering for the CEO position. Both Maxine and Edie had told me I was coming in at the end of LVMH's search process. At the same time, I was moving forward with my own search, because I realized that something great could still happen for me, whether it was the Donna Karan job or something else. I was newly confident that I knew the fashion business inside and out. Regardless of what questions anyone asked of me—whether it was Wall Street, how bankers evaluate investments in a company, or inventory management, or marketing, or design, or the U.S. model for business—I had the experience and training to answer those questions.

In other words, I knew my stuff. That was important to keep in mind, because I had lost some of that confidence when I was terminated. That's part of what goes wrong when you're let go or fired from a job: you forget who you are and how competent, skilled, talented, and experienced you are. You need to remember that again. The job search process is complicated, but it begs you to remember. And in my case, I did.

By the time I met with Mr. Belloni, I had two other designer opportunities. One was an offer that was about to be extended to me (and later was); the other was about to happen. I also had one or two other prospects that weren't in the designer world. Thus, I knew I was getting a job, and that gave me a certain degree of confidence. Again, however, just as with the 7 For All Mankind opportunity, I wasn't interested in working at a monobrand company. I came from a company where my energy level was very high, and I was accustomed to managing multiple brands and multiple businesses. Then it happened: he asked me to consider joining Donna Karan International, and I said, "I'm flattered that you would consider me for this job, but I must tell you that I have other considerations. If you would think about making me part of the LVMH group and you would offer me involvement with the group as a corporate officer, nobody would be able to compete with you and I would join the company."

In response, Mr. Belloni said, "What if I offered you Thomas Pink?" I said, "I'd be very interested." He then said, "Listen, Mark, I think you're a very good guy. I'm very interested in you. We're now talking about a bigger role in the group. Would you be willing to come to Paris next week and meet with me, the head of our human resources, and Mr. Bernard Arnault?"

I almost fell off my chair. I couldn't believe my good fortune in what he had just asked me. Bernard Arnault is the CEO, chairman, and founder of LVMH, which is arguably the finest luxury group in the world. Its luxury brand portfolio includes Berluti, Bulgari, Dior, Dom Perignon, Donna Karan, Fendi, Givenchy, Loro Piana, Marc Jacobs, Sephora, Tag Heuer, and Thomas Pink—more than 60 brands in total. He's also reputed to be the richest man in France and one of the richest men in the world. Somehow I kept a straight face when I calmly said, "Sure, I would make myself available to go to Paris." He said, "Thank you. I appreciate your time. We'll get back to you." And our conversation was over.

> I had lost some of that confidence when I was terminated. That's part of what goes wrong when you're let go or fired from a job: you forget who you are and how competent, skilled, talented, and experienced you are. You need to remember that again.

The next day I got a call from Edie Steinberg, who put me in touch with LVMH's travel group to make my arrangements to fly to Paris. The next week I flew to Paris, arriving the night before our meeting. I hadn't been to Paris in a while. LVMH had arranged for me to stay in the Hotel de la Tremoille, just around the corner and a few blocks from the LVMH corporate headquarters on Avenue Montaigne. As soon as I arrived, jet-lagged and rumpled, I walked from the hotel to the office complex: I wanted to make sure I knew how to get there and how long it would take. Then I wanted to visit the LVMH stores in the area. Before I went to Paris, I had visited several Donna Karan stores, a Louis Vuitton store, several Dior stores, and anything else I could find that would give me a better idea of the group.

I didn't sleep very well that night: I was jet-lagged, and I was naturally very excited. The next morning, I got up early, showered, shaved, put on my best navy blue suit and white shirt (which is my uniform), and walked to the LVMH offices to meet Bernard Arnault.

It was one of the greatest meetings of my life. I believe the secret to my success in that interview was that by that point in my job search I was absolutely fearless. I was thrilled to be there. I was confident because I had gotten this far. I knew my stuff—again, regardless of the subject, I was able to discuss it, because I was well trained and articulate. I believe people sense fear: they can tell whether you're comfortable or uncomfortable, and I was completely comfortable. I was so happy to be meeting this man, who is arguably the leader in luxury goods in the world, one of the world's most successful businessmen, with an amazing reputation and an extraordinary list of accomplishments.

Although the French seem very formal, I am not. I'm an American. I always have a big smile on my face. I am not afraid to ask questions, and I'm not afraid to answer them. His first question was excellent: "Tell me, Mark, what do you bring to a company?" My answer was equally excellent (if I do say so myself): "Energy. I bring energy." And it went on from there. In the end, our interview, which I believe was supposed to be only 10 or 15 minutes, lasted about 45 minutes: we just kept talking. I asked him dozens of questions about how he started, what he was interested in, and what he needed to do. In hindsight, I think I asked him more questions than he asked me. But I sensed that he liked me because I was confident, I was comfortable in my skin, and by the time I met with him, I felt he needed me more than I needed him. Remember, as I mentioned earlier, a company needs qualified people more than people need the company. You just need to know it.

Next, I met with the head of human resources for LVMH, Madame Concetta Lanciaux, who told me, "Mr. Arnault and Mr. Belloni like you very much. Tell me about yourself." She also asked me a series of probing questions. She was a very interesting lady and smart as a whip. Since then, I've learned that everyone at LVMH is smart: that's the price of entry. Everyone there is "worldly," because they're all involved in so many businesses in so many countries. I found myself dealing with people on a much higher level than I had ever dealt with before. Their businesses are diverse, ranging from newspapers to shipbuilding, fragrances and cosmetics, accessories, apparel, watches, and jewelry. Also, they sell in every market in the world. This company is the real deal.

My final meeting that day was with Mr. Belloni. As soon as I sat down, he said, "Mr. Arnault was taken with you. He enjoyed his conversation, as I did, with you. We think you are a very interesting candidate, and we'd like to make you an offer. Will you be available to meet with me next week if I fly to New York?" Again I said, "Absolutely." I flew home, shared with Maxine Martens and Edie Steinberg what had happened, and waited.

Two days later, I got the call: Mr. Belloni was coming to New York and wanted me to meet with him at the LVMH tower on West 57th Street. That was a meeting that meant more to me than I can express in words. We met in his office and Mr. Belloni began by reiterating how much he and Mr. Arnault enjoyed meeting me, and then he told me they wanted me to join the company to run Donna Karan International. He went on to say, "We want to do this with dignity. We want someone who joins us who has respect for the individuals who work here, who will work to understand the European culture, and who wants to work hard to make this successful. We think that might be you." Then he handed me the offer letter, and the first thing I read was "CEO LVMH Inc." I was so overwhelmed, I'm not sure my eyes focused on anything after that.

I read the list of responsibilities they were offering me:

- CEO of LVMH Inc.
- Member of the executive committee in Paris
- Chairman and CEO of Donna Karan
- Operational responsibility for Thomas Pink globally
- M&A management team in the United States

And the financial package was generous. I thought to myself, Oh, my gosh, this is amazing. I'm back. I said, "I accept. I can't tell you how grateful I am. *I will deliver this business for you.*"

What he said next took me by surprise: "You're not even going to negotiate? What about the financial package?" I said, "Money is not an issue. I accept your offer. I told you I wasn't coming here for money."

He looked at me and said, "Well, that doesn't work for me. You're going to start in the middle of the year, so I am going to guarantee your bonus on a prorated basis for the first year." I interrupted him: "You really don't have to do this." But he continued: "We need you to do a big job for us, so we want you focused on the business, not the money. We want to make sure that's not an issue." I thought I had just learned an important lesson in management, my first as part of the group. P.S.: I eventually told the group I would have worked for free! We shook hands, and that was how the next phase of my career began. I was happy, relieved, vindicated, and proud—not only because this was a terrific opportunity at the world's leading luxury-goods company, not only because I would be responsible for some truly great brands, and not only because I believed I could take the businesses I would be running to even higher levels of success. I was also happy because I had waited for the right opportunity to come along; I hadn't simply jumped at the first opportunity that came my way—not that there was anything wrong with any of the companies I had interviewed with or the positions I had put on hold while I waited for this final meeting. I'd had the strength and intestinal fortitude to wait.

When Mr. Belloni offered me this job, I thought of a friend who always said when something good happened to him, "I'm bald, and I don't deserve that, but I deserve *this*." I felt the same way. I didn't deserve to be let go, but life worked out, and I deserved this wonderful opportunity to join LVMH. When you're down, everybody always tells you that things will work out for the best; my sons, Jarrod and Jesse, also kept telling me: "You're going to do better. Just wait." And now here I was: I had just joined the finest luxury company in the world, with a title bigger than I knew what to do with. I was so proud. That was what I felt: proud. It was such a happy moment for me.

It was an even happier moment when I told my family, which I didn't do for a few weeks. I've always been very reluctant to tell my family anything about my career until it's a done deal. Since I knew we still had a few weeks' worth of final negotiations, I didn't want them to know I had gotten the offer. I wanted to surprise them, which was really hard for me to do. I told them only that LVMH was working on a proposal for me and that I was pretty sure I was going to get the job.

Two weeks later, just before July 4, I took my family to lunch at my favorite restaurant in Manhattan. I had a copy of the offer letter to be signed. I brought the contract back to the restaurant, put it in front of my wife, and said, "I have something I want you to read." It listed the same responsibilities that I had read in Mr. Belloni's office a few weeks earlier, beginning with "CEO of LVMH." Then we celebrated: what a great July Fourth that was!

But was it? Unknown to me, there still was Donna's sign-off.

Many of you reading this may think I was lucky to get this job, but I truly believe that the harder I work, the luckier I get. I also believe there are some valuable lessons here for anyone who's looking for a new job, or a better position, or a promotion: Recognize that you have something to offer. Don't be intimidated. If you lose your job, you're going to go through a process that's not easy. It's hurtful, and it's devastating. Admittedly, I was fortunate, but the entire time I was going through my job search, I often thought of people who are not as fortunate. I'm grateful for everything I have today. Moreover, I do everything I can to help others when they lose their jobs, because I know I'm in a position in which I can offer opportunities for them to meet people who might hire them. I also understand how to organize and how to approach the search challenge. I believe this process is more beneficial than the introductions I can make. I learned the hard way how to approach a job search. But as a person who hires people and as a person who had to find a job, I believe my counsel is worth listening to.

Also, I realize I'm fortunate that my job search lasted only four months: I was let go in March, and I had the offer from LVMH by July 1. I know many people today who have been out of work for much longer than that, in some cases for years. The economists call these people long-term unemployed, and some politicians claim that many are no longer looking for work. I believe that's not true, and my heart goes out to anyone who doesn't have a job and wants one. I know how fortunate I was that I didn't have to worry about where my next dollar or my next meal would come from; nevertheless, the job search is still a very humbling experience.

That's why I think that when you're looking for a job, the first thing you need to do is recognize—and accept—that it's not going to be pleasant. You're going to go through a period in which you experience a wide variety of negative emotions: anger, denial, discomfort, unhappiness, worry. But if you've been successful in a previous job and believe you have something to offer another company, I think you'll find another job. It may take time, but you'll get placed again. You just have to have confidence and believe in your training.

Then call everyone you know and let them all know you're actively and hungrily looking for work. Many people make the mistake of not wanting to broadcast that they're out of work: they think it's something to be ashamed of. But in this economy it can happen to anyone, and it does. You need to work your network, however small or large it is, and start calling. You'll be surprised (as I was) who comes through for you. Sometimes people you haven't talked to or heard from in years will be very happy to hear from you: if you had a good relationship with them or earned their respect, that doesn't go away no matter how many years have gone by. Don't talk yourself out of making those calls!

Also, think about who your contacts might know and what companies you're interested in working for and ask the people you're calling if you can call or e-mail their contacts. Don't wait for someone to make the introduction: as well intentioned as many people are, they're also busy, and some are forgetful. Also, they don't have the urgency that you have when you're looking for work. Ask them if you can call or e-mail their contacts directly so that they don't have to do anything except give you contact information. Follow up, of course, with everyone who helps you: a thank-you note or e-mail goes a long way and will be appreciated and remembered by everyone you send one to.

No matter what, start making phone calls. Call people you're not comfortable calling. Remember, there's no lead—and no job—that's too small and none that's too big. Get your foot in the door first and then decide whether you want any position you interview for. Be willing to meet anyone and take anyone's help, wherever it comes from. Don't be afraid to ask for help. Put your ego aside and look for work. Get organized and plan your days, then *work that plan*.

Finally, you have to be willing to recalibrate in terms of what you're earning, or your job responsibilities, or your title. You have to be willing to take a step back in title or position. That doesn't mean you *will* do that, but you have to *be willing* to. Don't let your ego get in your way.

25

"I Think You'd Be
Great for Dior"

Although I had an understanding with LVMH, Donna Karan personally had input into the decision about who would be the next chairman and CEO of Donna Karan International. LVMH arranged for us to meet, but the only possible time was July 14–15 because I had planned a family vacation to San Diego and we were leaving on July 15. Donna has a compound on Parrot Cay Island, which is part of the Turks and Caicos Islands in the Caribbean, and I agreed to fly there en route to my vacation. I took a plane from New York to Miami, another plane from Miami to the Turks and Caicos, and then a boat to Parrot Cay.

The boat was a cabin cruiser, and it was a beautiful day, and I decided to stay on the back deck to admire the view and enjoy the sunshine. Everyone else chose to go inside. I was wearing a white T-shirt, white cargo pants, white sneakers, and mirrored Ray-Ban aviators, which is what I usually wear when I'm traveling to a beach. The reason I mention all this is that I soon found out why everyone else had gone inside: I was drenched by waves the entire trip. It didn't bother me, since it was a hot and sunny day and I figured I would have time to change before meeting Donna.

When the boat docked, I was surprised to find Donna herself waiting for me in a golf cart. Moreover, she wasn't there to whisk me away to my hotel but to take me to her home, where the managing director of LVMH, Mr. Antonio Belloni, was already waiting so that we could have lunch and begin our meeting. I couldn't believe I didn't have a chance to clean up, and I was a bit self-conscious because I was soaked through and looked a bit like something the cat dragged in. But there was nothing I could do, and so I made the best of it. At least Donna and

Mr. Belloni were also casually dressed, and so if I hadn't been soaked, I would have fit right in. But I'm getting ahead of the story.

When I got off the boat and into her golf cart, she said, "You look so familiar." I said, "Donna, that's because you and I interviewed a few years ago. Don't you remember? I met your husband and your daughter, too. We spent many hours together talking about whether I should join your company." It was clear she had absolutely no recollection. I didn't mean to put her on the spot; I was just being honest that we had met before. I always thought I was hard to forget!

I had indeed met Donna once before. In 1996, when I was vice chairman of PVH and had just acquired Izod and Gant, I received a call from Marnie McBride, a headhunter I had known for several years. She told me that Donna Karan International was looking for a CEO, and would I be interested in talking to them? Until that call, I had never considered leaving PVH, because I was happy with the company and with my career: I was always treated fairly. Remember, I'd had 25 assignments in 25 years: I kept being given additional responsibilities, and so my work was always interesting and challenging as I moved up the ladder. Also, I took great pride that I had started at PVH in an entry-level job yet was proving that I could get to the top by working at a single company. Although people called me all the time about various opportunities, I never considered any of them, and I never went on interviews.

But Donna Karan International was a great company: it's a world-class brand, recognizable by everyone, and was in another industry, which included both women's and men's fashion. I felt it would be a very interesting, high-profile opportunity for me, maybe even a transforming opportunity, and so when I got the call, I agreed to a meeting.

I had an interview at the 21 Club with Mr. Bill Benedetto, the lead director on the Donna Karan board. We talked a great deal about the business, and my training took over. He believed I had the skills needed to be their CEO, and he wanted to introduce me to Donna's husband, Stephan Weiss. A few nights later I met him at their apartment. Stephan talked about wanting to find someone for the company who would ensure that the brand would stand the test of time. I found that fascinating because it had never occurred to me that in addition to fame and fortune, one of the most important things to designers is for their legacy to live on. I remember he said he was looking for a "soul mate" for Donna, and I thought that was a bit odd but insightful. This was five years before Stephan died of lung cancer, and he may have been looking for someone to help with Donna's legacy because he knew he didn't have long to live: I can't say for sure, but that occurred to me in retrospect.

After I talked to Stephan, Donna and her daughter came home, and we all had a brief conversation. I subsequently had a follow-up interview with Donna at the office of the headhunter. We had a great conversation, after which I believed I was going to have to make a serious decision about whether to leave PVH to join Donna Karan.

Soon after those conversations, Bruce, the CEO of PVH, asked me to have lunch. Remember, Bruce had been my first boss, and we had worked together for more than 20 years at that point and were friends. As we walked up Madison Avenue, Bruce said, "I have a problem. I was offered a job, and I need your advice as to whether I should take it or not."

I asked him if it paid a lot of money, and when he said yes and told me how much, I told him he should take the job. Then I asked him what company it was, and he said, "Donna Karan." With that, we walked into the restaurant. I knew there was no way he had interviewed for the same job I had, but I didn't know how he could have found out I had talked to Donna and her husband. I just waited to see what would happen next.

After we ordered, he looked across the table and said, "I'm going to make you president of the corporation. We've been doing this together for a very long time. There's no one in the world I trust more than you. You've never let me down. You've never let the company down. Anything we've given you has worked, so I want you to become the president. However, I need to convince the board that we need a president, so I need you to have a little patience over the next few months."

That was Bruce's way of telling me that he knew I was interviewing and didn't want me to leave. He wanted me to know that if I stayed, I would be promoted to president of the corporation. I was flabbergasted, grateful, and excited, but I didn't understand why it would take a few months. He said, "I need to convince the board, so just bear with me." Over the next six months, I was heavily involved with G.H. Bass & Co., which was in dire straits and which we reorganized completely. During that time, Donna Karan International hired someone else to be its CEO. And in March 1997, I not only became president of the company, I was also given a seat on the board, which was completely unexpected.

As fate would have it, a year later I was the president of the company, and Bruce and I were having lunch at Michael's on 55th Street. One of the directors on our board, Peter Solomon, who is a very well-known investment banker in New York City, happened to be having lunch at the same restaurant, and he stopped by our table to say hello to Bruce and me. With him was one of his friends whom he apparently had known for quite some time, and he introduced him to Bruce and me. His name was Bill Benedetto. I looked at Bruce across the table and said, "So that's how you found out."

I wrote earlier that it used to be a badge of honor to work for one company. In today's world, however, no matter how well you're doing in your company, it's always a good idea to peek out of your cubbyhole. In my case, if I hadn't had the opportunity in 1996 to interview on the outside at Donna Karan International, I wouldn't have known how much I meant to PVH. That promotion reinforced my belief that when you handle yourself well within your company and your company likes you, if you receive an offer on the outside, your company will fight to keep you. That offer could change your life as it did mine, because your company will give you increased responsibility or a higher salary, because when a company invests in people, it doesn't want to lose them. Nevertheless, years later, when I met with Donna again, I thought it was almost fate that the one company I had interviewed with was now considering me again—and it turned out to be the company I ended up with. Whatever it was that drew me to Donna Karan International, maybe it was just meant to be. But I'm getting ahead of the story.

So here I was meeting Donna again 10 years later. We were still on the dock where I had disembarked from the boat to Parrot Cay when she asked me where her packages were. Before I left New York to meet her, Patti Cohen, who was the executive VP of marketing and PR for Donna Karan International, had called to ask if I would take several packages to her on Parrot Cay. She said it was mostly business materials (which obviously implied that it wasn't *only* business materials but also some personal things she wanted), and she estimated that they weighed about 20 or 25 pounds. I refused. I couldn't believe anyone was even asking me to do this, and I thought, I'm not her mule. I was on vacation, and I was taking only carry-on luggage, and if I had taken her packages, I would have needed to check my luggage, which I didn't want to do. When Donna asked for her packages and I told her I hadn't brought them, she asked why, and I said I didn't want to. Now it was clear that she wasn't happy.

After I was hired, Patti asked me why I had refused to take them, knowing how irritated Donna would be. Obviously, taking them to Donna might have put me in her good graces. But I had already been informed that she was looking for someone with a strictly luxury background, and I wasn't it, and so I decided if I let her walk all over me, that wouldn't help me win her over anyway. I knew she had a strong point of view, and I needed to establish strength for me personally and for the company. I believe that anyone who shows weakness is already in trouble. As I said earlier, I had to be strong to earn her respect; my experience, talent, and business acumen would go only so far. I wouldn't be able to do that if I agreed to act as her errand boy and luggage carrier. I believed I needed to establish some ground rules for our relationship because I knew I was what she needed to grow her business, and I had to find a way to convince her of that.

When we arrived at Donna's house, I noticed immediately that everything was impeccable: every piece of furniture, every painting and statue, every carpet and curtain, everything down to the pebbles on the path to her door, was absolutely exquisite and perfect. I had never seen something so well designed and well executed in any museum, hotel, or private home. I've never seen anything like it before (or since), which only proved further her impeccable taste and what talented, creative people she had chosen to surround herself in business and in her personal life to build and furnish this lovely sanctuary on the waterfront of this gorgeous island.

Parrot Cay also has a Four Seasons Hotels resort that services the few houses on the island, and our lunch was being served by the hotel. It was beautifully laid out on a table, but before we sat down, Donna threw me for a loop when she asked, "Why don't we have our meeting in the pool?" In the pool? I said, "I'm not wearing a bathing suit, and it *is* our first meeting, and I think for a business meeting as important as this we should be in a setting other than a swimming pool, Donna." So that was how we started: we didn't exactly hit it off right away.

Fortunately, I had given a lot of thought to my strategy for handling this meeting. I had decided to treat her like a hostile witness, the way lawyers sometimes do in court. I did that because I was warned that Donna did not want me to be the CEO of her company. I knew she wanted someone from the luxury world, but I also knew that she and LVMH had tried this approach with the previous three CEOs (in six years), and although I'm sure all three were very smart and talented, none of them had worked out. I had been warned beforehand that because I wasn't from the world of luxury, Donna was going to be less than happy about my candidacy.

Additionally, I had done my homework, as anyone should do in an interview. Before this meeting I had visited every single department store in my geographic area—New York, New Jersey, and Connecticut—that I thought would carry Donna Karan products. I visited her freestanding stores and any store that sold Donna Karan or DKNY to get a sense of what they looked like. I read all the brochures and all the information that had been supplied to me by the search firms and LVMH, and I read all the articles I could find about Donna Karan: what the company was looking for and what was important to her. Interestingly, when I visited the stores, I noticed they weren't at all what I expected them to be, lacking in terms of designs, product mix, display, or presentation, but I was hesitant to share those impressions with Donna.

The three of us sat down to lunch, and I had barely settled into my seat when Donna asked, "So, Mark, why do you think you should be the CEO of this company?" I said, "Well, Donna, I can tell you that in everything I've done in my career, I've had a track record that shows that I'm able to accomplish what the tasks are. I had 25 assignments in my prior company that covered every facet of running a retail and wholesale business. And I have intense experience in the collection business, having bought the Calvin Klein Company, where I was the managing director overseeing it. So I have deep brand experience and designer experience, which I think earmarks me perfectly for this job.

"Also, as I understand it, you had some very good people as previous CEOs—a retailer, a successful entrepreneur who had managed Giorgio Armani, and most recently a corporate attorney who had been involved with Marc Jacobs—but for whatever reason, they didn't work out. I think it's time you brought in a serious guy who has *hands-on* business experience and who has proved he understands all the disciplines. I began as a designer. I've been involved in sourcing. I've managed and overseen a wide variety of different opportunities and brands. I think there aren't many things I haven't done. I think you'll determine today whether I'm smart, but I can tell you, I know I'm well trained."

Then she asked, "What do you think about retail?" I said, "I believe retail is the future. I think having your own stores is the way to represent your brand in the best possible light, to reflect the way you envision your brand. When you have your own stores, you're in total control over your environment, so you can make sure your presentations are as sharp as they can be. You can make sure the messages you want will get across to your customers. And because retail is vertical, that's the best way to maximize your profits."

Her next question was, "What do you think about my stores?" I didn't really want to answer her, at least not this early in our conversation, because what I had observed wasn't really positive. I simply said, "I visited your stores, but I looked at them only briefly. I wasn't there to examine your stores and determine what was right or wrong about them." Donna didn't want to let go of the topic, and so she asked me, "You were in my stores, and you have nothing to say about them?" Again I tried to avoid the subject by simply saying, "Yes, I visited them, and I'm sure there are many good things about them." At this point I saw clearly that I had hit a nerve.

She moved on to another subject and asked me what I thought about the collection business, which is the top of the pyramid in the brand portfolio and strategy. I told her, "I really admire the collection business. I know you began with collection. I have a great understanding of it. It's challenging to make money at it, but I think it's a very, very important component of the business because it's the one that allows all the goodwill to spill over into everything else you do in your pyramid, namely, DKNY and DKNY jeans."

Then she said, "I understood you didn't like the collection business at Calvin Klein." (Someone from Calvin Klein had spoken to her out of turn. I found out later who it was; this should not have happened.) I countered this by telling her that the collection business at Calvin Klein was a smaller component of the company as a whole, whereas in Donna Karan International, collection is a major component of the business. The Donna Karan Collection has really talented people who have built the business to a very impressive size, with the best distribution at department stores around the world, and I am in awe of the product.

She also tried to talk to me about fashion, women's fashion, which was new to me. She asked me what I thought about women's wear and what kind of designs I liked. I avoided those questions, too: after all, at that point in my career I was new to women's wear, and so I wasn't going to get into a debate about fashion with Donna Karan, one of the world's greatest designers. I'd have had to be out of my mind to do that.

Essentially, with every subject she brought up, I refused to debate her, because it was clear she wasn't trying to find common ground. She wasn't trying to hire me; she was trying to unhire me. I subsequently learned that she wanted to prove that because I didn't come from a luxury brand, I wasn't right for her company. Finally, I said, "Donna, the business isn't working. The company's not making the required returns. The parent company is unhappy with the results. It's reluctant to invest in the future because you need stronger leadership. I can provide that: I've been there and done it all, I've been successful in what I've done, and I'm not sitting here for personal gain. I'm not here for money. I'm not here for corporate politics. Been there, done that. I'm here to work and be productive. In this, I'm pure of heart."

That was how our first meeting ended. After Donna left, Mr. Belloni took me aside and asked me, "What are you doing? You're not answering her questions." I explained, "I'll tell you what I'm doing. First, I'm not going to let her walk all over me. Second, I *am* answering the questions, but I'm not going to fall into a trap where she proves to you or to herself that I can't handle managing a business that frankly I am convinced there's nobody better than me to do for you." Mr. Belloni seemed unconvinced, but he let the conversation drop for the time being.

Later, after I finally had an opportunity to check in at my hotel, Donna, Mr. Belloni, and I met for dinner. It was a lovely candlelit meal on an open portico with a wood-slatted roof so that we could sit outside. There were full-length drapes floating in the breeze, and I couldn't imagine a more beautiful setting. It should have been one of the most wonderful nights of my life; instead, I was very uncomfortable. Donna again was posing questions to illustrate that I didn't know what I was doing, and so it was time to push back. You know, companies often hire executives from other industries. They believe expertise in management carries over. Leadership works. However, I was from *this* industry.

Finally, I said, "Let's talk about product. You know, Donna, when I went into the collection store, I found the product awe-inspiring. But when I went into the department stores that sell your brands, I've got to tell you, with all the assortments of products you have and all the stores you're in, I wasn't inspired at all. I saw some great stuff and a lot of filler, stuff you're not going to win awards for, and I was disappointed by that."

At that point Mr. Belloni was mostly listening: he knew this conversation needed to be between Donna and me.

I took this aggressive approach with Donna in our second meeting because it was important to have a point of view. One of my credos is lead, follow, or get out of the way, and that afternoon I was willing to take her punches and willing to sit back and listen. But when she started to press me again, I felt she needed to hear what I really thought. As a result, our dinner conversation was better not only because I was no longer silent but also because we were truly discussing issues affecting the business and the brands.

Some of what she heard was uncomfortable to hear, but at the end of each difficult conversation I tried very hard to soften the blow: I repeatedly told her, "Donna, the company needs a businessperson to run it. I accept that you have the greatest designers and the greatest retail people, but it seems to me they need leadership and someone who can pull everything together and someone who can push back. So if a delivery is late, somebody can ask why and understand, or if they can't get the prices they want, there's somebody who knows how to solve that problem. I believe you've had some great people, but none of them knew how to run the business at the in-depth level that I can."

And with that, dinner was over. Obviously, I can't say what she thought of me at that point; all I can comment on is what I said and did.

After dinner, I had a quick wrap-up with Mr. Belloni, who told me he wasn't sure I had handled the conversation in the right way but he was willing to see what happened. He was leaving the next morning, when I would be meeting for a third time with Donna, alone.

The next morning Donna and I met after breakfast, at eleven after her yoga session, and we had what I thought was a great meeting. I told her, "I have nothing but the highest regard for you. I can't imagine how complicated it was for you to achieve what you achieved. You are one of the most successful people in the world, and in particular in the industry we're in, and I admire everything you have accomplished. I believe you know what you need to do to make this company incredible for the future. *This brand is bigger than the business.* I know how to run a company. Whatever is wrong with this company, I can fix, and I can build on what's good. I have the discipline, the experience, and the business savvy from having fixed companies. I was the go-to guy in my last company for 30 years: whenever we made an acquisition, whenever there was a business that needed to be fixed, I was the guy who did it. I began in design and have worked in sourcing, operations, planning, retail, wholesale, everything: you name it, I've done it. I can fix this company.

I'm also very strong-willed, and I'm not afraid to make tough decisions. I'm willing to work with the people you have in place if they're good, and you say they are. I'm the guy who can come in and solidify all the businesses."

I saw she was finally listening because now it was just the two of us and I was able to tell her myself what I could do for the company. Our conversation lasted for about an hour: it was great. I felt we were bonding: I was so in touch with her at that point. I was seeing us as friends and business associates. I really liked her. But I had to go catch a plane. Before we parted, she suggested that I get my luggage and she would pick me up and take me to the boat.

This brand is bigger than the business. I know how to run a company. Whatever is wrong with this company, I can fix, and I can build on what's good. I have the discipline, the experience, and the business savvy.

A few minutes later she drove up in a golf cart. As we drove to the boat, she said to me, "I've thought about what you said, Mark. You're a great guy, and I really like you. You've convinced me that you really know the business, and I am really glad that we spent this time together." Then, just as we pulled up to the boat, she said, "I think you'd be great for Dior."

"You think I'd be great for Dior? That's what you say to me after all this? I give up. I don't know what else to say to you, Donna, except I did have a good time hanging out with you."

And I left.

I got on the plane and headed out to Southern California to meet my family. I was in a great mood: Parrot Cay was amazing. I figured Donna would come around. The company had had people with luxury experience, and it had people from other backgrounds; now it had an opportunity to bring in a practical guy with a great track record. This should have been an easy decision for her, and so I wasn't concerned. I was ready for the next chapter.

26

The
Media Barrage

The day after I arrived in Southern California, I was playing golf at the Aviara Golf Club in San Diego with my sons. It's a beautiful setting, and I was enjoying spending time with my family, when I received a call from Madame Concetta, LVMH's head of human resources at that time. I had barely said hello when she started berating me: "How *dare* you talk to the press? We at LVMH do *not* share our private discussions. We are very careful when we make announcements; we *choose* when we decide to release information. We don't have other people speak on our behalf—let alone people who don't even work for the company!"

I was stunned. I said, "Madame Concetta, with all due respect, I don't know what you're talking about." She told me there was an article in the press about my meeting with Donna Karan in Parrot Cay. When I heard that, I said, "Madame Concetta, you're talking to the wrong person. I didn't even know there was an article. I suggest you go back to Donna Karan and her vast PR network and talk to them." Then I called a friend to find out what she was talking about.

Over the last year, there had been a series of articles in various media stating that LVMH was looking for someone to take the lead at DKI, and there had been many rumors about the future of Donna Karan. My name had never been mentioned, though, until this article appeared in *Women's Wear Daily*, which very clearly stated something along the lines of "Donna Karan will never work with Mark Weber." As my friend read me the article, I realized the article itself was even worse than the headline (if that was possible) because it also said something like "Not sure why LVMH would be interested in Mark Weber after he was let go as CEO of PVH after only eight months." (The truth was, I was acting CEO for more than 15 months.) But that was a problem: I was worried about how Mr. Arnault and Mr. Belloni would react after reading it.

The next morning, at the golf course, I called one of the senior people at *Women's Wear Daily,* a very accomplished person with whom I had become acquainted over the years. He was gracious enough to take my call, and I said, "I don't know whether or not you're following what's going on with me and LVMH and Donna Karan International, but yesterday your publication ran an article that included what seemed to be a personal attack. I've read your newspaper my entire life, and I've never seen comments about anyone like what I read about me. It almost seems like the paper is trying to say that I don't deserve to work ever again. I have a 30-year history in the industry. It's true that PVH let me go, but the filings with the SEC clarified that there was no wrongdoing on my part. These things happen, and while I wasn't happy about it, it's just a fact of life. If the management of LVMH is interested in hiring me and they read this statement, can you imagine what signal this article is sending?"

He said, "Mark, I appreciate your call, and although I will not say that my reporter has done anything wrong, I will take a closer look at what was written. And if this is covered in the future, I will make sure the coverage is fair."

That evening I got a call from Madame Concetta, who apologized and told me she had found out I was not the one who leaked the story. A small win.

Unfortunately, once a story like that was out there, there wasn't much I could do about it. There's no retracting an article; even if a publication issues "corrections," people typically don't read them, and so the damage was done. Donna's comment stating that she would never work with me was a major problem, and the paper's questioning why LVMH would consider hiring me was frightening.

I remember someone once telling me, "You never want to get in a fight with people who buy ink by the barrel." I wasn't looking to get in a fight with *Women's Wear Daily* or with the famous Donna Karan. I also realize that not everyone has access to the senior people of an industry publication, and I want to be clear that I didn't influence anyone in any way on what they wrote about me—before or after that article. I simply wanted to be treated as they had treated others in my situation. I had the wherewithal and intelligence to confront a massive problem with the press and to take at least some action. I can't say whether it worked or didn't work, but I think it shows that even with the press, when you're right, you're right, and when you're wrong, you're wrong.

Unfortunately, the story doesn't end there. I was hoping to have a quick decision and an early start date after returning from my vacation, but communication went dark. I knew most European companies take the month of August for vacation, but this was still July, and even if they were on vacation, I thought I would at least find out where I stood.

But I heard absolutely nothing: complete radio silence!

Right before August 1, I e-mailed Mr. Belloni and asked where we stood. He said, "It looks like we're going to delay a while. It's summer, people are on vacation, so let's regroup in September." I was not happy. I was troubled and concerned, to say the least. In my mind, I had a job; I was planning strategy, next steps, and travel ideas, when *boom*! Silence. I had taken the summer off, but I still had all this uncertainty with LVMH. (I did get my handicap down to 10: not working does wonders for your golf game but not for your head.)

Then, during the first week of September, Mr. Belloni called me and said, "Out of respect for Donna, we're continuing to look for people. She has several people she's interested in, whom I'm going to interview. We believe you're the right guy for the job, but we think this is the proper way to handle this situation."

Que sera sera: what will be, will be.

I started to plan a coast-to-coast vacation, but I was uncomfortable. I was in limbo. I recognized, perhaps for the first time, that I was dealing with a different culture and I had much to learn. This was an unusual place for me to be: the highs, the lows.

I knew they were interviewing, but I didn't know anything else. It's difficult to be happy when you're concerned that everything might not work out as well as you thought it was going to. Sometime in the fall, *WWD* wrote an article titled "Dunno Karan." It was rumored that if DK didn't hire Mark Weber, they didn't know who would run that company. There was no end in sight to the CEO search. Finally, after my exit from PVH, I had a positive statement and some positive momentum!

At the end of September, I got an e-mail from LVMH that simply said, "We'd like to talk." When we did, I found out they had exhausted all other possibilities for this position and wanted Donna and me to reconnect. LVMH set up a private meeting between us at Donna's apartment in New York, and I told her, "Donna, this lack of leadership is taking a toll on everyone. I can fix your company. If you want this company to grow, to be what it could be, and to stand the test of time, I can do it. I give you my word that I'll do everything possible to make it work. I'll keep you in the loop. I'll make you a partner in everything I do. We can learn from each other and agree to respect each other."

And she said, "We're going to do this." So it was decided: we were going to work together.

When we made the announcement to the press, Donna said, "Sometimes a first date doesn't work." That was the headline for the announcement. Finally, I was officially hired! I started on October 15, 2006, two and a half months after the date I thought I would begin. My role was to figure out what we needed to do together to make her brand as big as it should have been. I had a plan for how to do that, and I had the tenacity and confidence to execute that plan.

While I was waiting for LVMH and Donna to make their decision, I never considered looking for another position. I was committed to LVMH, and I thought they were committed to me. By the time I interviewed with LVMH, I knew I would find something meaningful. Moreover, I believed LVMH needed me. That goes back to what Maxine Martens asked me before she connected me to LVMH: "Who needs you?" I convinced the LVMH group that I was right for them; all I had to do was convince Donna Karan.

Moreover, waiting until Donna came around to LVMH's view of who should be the next CEO of the DKI company was the right thing to do. It was LVMH's decision to make, and they were entitled to do whatever they needed to do before hiring anyone. I had faith that the system would work, and I don't believe in pushing people to make decisions when they're not ready to make them. Because they won't. If anyone ever comes to me with anything and says, "I must have an answer now," my answer is always no. I—and you—have a right to think, to consider, before making important decisions. This doesn't make you indecisive; it allows you to make the right decision.

I believe there are some valuable takeaways here. First and foremost, I stood my ground and followed my view, vision, and position on what was important and relevant. I had the presence of mind to never waver in my stance. I remained confident, calm, and professional. I was incredibly respectful of and cooperative with all parties involved. It is not my company; I was asking for a seat at their table. They set the rules and the timetables. They had a tremendous respect for the founder and creative director's point of view. LVMH was patient but definitive when they made decisions. None of this was personal; it was strictly business. (What movie is that from?) I was committed, and I hoped they were, too. I trusted the system. As my wife said, "What will be, will be. Let's enjoy the summer." She is always right. My sons were the best: they knew I would land well. Family and friends help you stay focused. They help you put things in perspective. I wanted to work for LVMH probably more than any goal in my career. Yet I did what I could do. The decision was out of my hands.

That said, I'm not sure the same strategy applies for everyone in other types or levels of work. Other people in similar situations may not want to wait it out, especially if they're interviewing for a lower-level position or if they can't afford to wait. If you find yourself in that situation and you know you've done everything you can, there comes a time when you might want to start looking for another position. Sometimes hiring decisions don't work out the way you think they will even when everyone has the best intentions, and so you need to protect yourself. Keep looking, and if you get another offer, you can come back to the company you really want to work for and let them know, and then they have to decide whether they want to hire you.

The Best Is Yet to Come

27

From Madison Avenue to Paris

My first official trip to Paris was in June 2006. Much had been going on. I focused my attention on the strategic plan for Donna Karan International, as directed and requested by the group. I integrated myself into the Thomas Pink business, which was based in London—what a great brand and great company. I truly enjoyed this opportunity, and my extensive shirt background made it relatively easy for me to contribute. The Thomas Pink CEO was Jonathan Heilbron, whose background was in finance, and he was good in his role: he knew the numbers. We complemented each other's skills, and I enjoyed this respite from the drama of Seventh Avenue.

I spent time in the tower. I had an office on the executive floor, learning about the group functions, including legal, human resources, real estate, and other administrative functions. It was the best of times. I viewed myself as an American in Paris (which I'll talk more about later) and was the standard-bearer for American businessmen. Often Europeans in general think of American executives as pampered, over-paid, and arrogant. I was determined to show a different side. I made it clear up front that money was not an issue. I was paid more than fairly, and my overall earning potential was spectacular. I wasn't interested in the politics. I wasn't going to Paris to compete. I had no illusions about being the next CEO. Frankly, I'd been there, done it, didn't need it, and it was not in the cards. I was happy to be in the United States. What was interesting was that I was making a name for myself as a good guy within the group. I was clearly different from many other Americans, who were often interested in their own personal gain rather than the needs of the company. I was determined to focus on the job, not on myself. Ask what you can do for your company. My discussions with the LVMH team were always on point, direct, and insightful and always about the company, not about me.

I noticed that any time people from France came to New York, they asked to come by and meet me. This brought to mind my earliest trips to Shanghai. I was in one of the first waves from the West after China was opened. When I ventured out into the streets, the people swarmed around me and stared, and some even touched me. They had never seen Westerners. I was treated as *foreign*, like an alien or the Creature from the Black Lagoon. I felt a little like that at LVMH: every week some new European or French executive would come by to meet or view me. Don't get me wrong: it was very flattering and also entertaining and interesting to observe. But even more important, I was breaking through. People were telling people I was someone they should meet, engage with, and offer a relationship and collaboration.

In my first few months I met everyone. I continued to develop a strategic plan with the proper sign-offs from Paris. I enlisted an outside consultant I knew, Mark Kerback, to help me prepare and work closely with the management team at DKI to get buy-in. Managing is an interesting phenomenon. You must manage to a number of constituents, not only the people who work for you. You need to consider or understand those constituents. You manage upward, to your boss or superiors, corporate office, and board. You manage your direct reports and hope to have them sign off on direction as your teammates. You must manage down to the executives at all levels of the organization: you want them fighting the good fight, by your side and believing that the direction you set is right. You manage to the outside, to your partners, licensees, and suppliers: you want and need them to believe in you and your company's direction. And of course, you need your customers to be excited about what you're doing. All in all, managing to these constituencies makes for success. I recognized this, and I made it happen. Hence, I was building respect and trust within the group.

In June 2006, I was in Paris the night before my first strategic meeting with LVMH. I had arranged to meet with Jean-Jacques Guiony, the LVMH CFO. He's a special guy: incredibly smart—I mean *scary* smart—and he knows the business. He's there because he deserves to be there. I shared with him the status of the business and the key points of the strategy he would be hearing about the next day. He gave me a few insights and asked questions I might not have considered. I was building goodwill with the senior financial guy in the group.

The next morning I had breakfast with Madame Concetta, head of human resources. I hadn't seen her since our infamous phone calls. She told me she was hearing wonderful things about me. That was a great way to start the day. We were having a wonderful conversation, when she asked me to move to Paris. I laughed, told her I was flattered, and of course I would move to Paris except that it was the wrong time for me and DKI. I was hired to make this work, I needed more time, and doing that was best for the group. She said she understood. To this day, I don't know if she was speaking for herself or for the group. She subsequently retired, and maybe when she reads this, she'll reach out to me. I found her to be very smart, confident, and expert.

While I'm on the subject of Concetta, about a year later I read in *Women's Wear Daily* that Concetta was stepping down but remaining on as an advisor to the group. I was quite disappointed to read this. I had all these fancy titles, I was building a relationship with LVMH, and I had to find out that she was leaving by reading it in the papers? I was unhappy and wanted to call this out, but I didn't. Instead, I waited.

About a month later, I was in a car talking with a senior executive of LVMH, and I shared how disappointed I was to learn of Madame Concetta's retirement in the paper. He turned to me and said, "We are a European company. Our culture is different. You must learn our culture. It will not change for you." This was not said in a negative way; it was just informative, a lesson to be learned. "And by the way, Mark, that's how I found out, too."

Back to June 2006. I finished my breakfast with Concetta. It was a great feeling to be so accepted. I walked to the LVMH tower and was escorted to the boardroom. Because it was still so early, 8:15 a.m., I was the first to arrive for the setup. I had not been in the boardroom during my interview, and so this was a first. The room was impressive in size and scope. All the shades were drawn on this beautiful sunny morning in Paris, and so I found the electronic switch and pressed it. This long 50-foot sweep of window shades started to open, revealing a breathtaking view of Paris and the Eiffel Tower with the sun shining down. I was overwhelmed, and I admit tears came to my eyes. I thought of the PVH business life that I had lost and realized that I had a new and even more exciting life. Here I was: from Brooklyn to Paris. The hardest math to master is learning to count your blessings. I was grateful.

The strategic plan was approved. The day and presentation were enriching, and all left with a plan, a mission, and a goal for the future. I continued to meet more and more of my European and global counterparts, but they stopped staring and began sharing. I was a teammate.

28

I Like to Think My Gray Hair Brings Wisdom

Back to my first day on the job. I joined LVMH and Donna Karan International in October 2006, following a whirlwind series of meetings. First I went to the LVMH tower, where I was introduced to the corporate staff as the CEO of LVMH Inc. Then I was whisked away to the DKI offices on Seventh Avenue in midtown Manhattan. I was very careful about how I intended to integrate myself into the company. Even though I was the chairman and CEO, I didn't want to come in with a heavy hand or behave as if I knew it all or had all the answers. If I hadn't been interested in people's input, I believe I would have soured the relationship immediately and not been successful. This is important for anyone who has ever been brought in to a company to implement change. Change is difficult for many people: during my career I've found that everybody wants change until you ask *him or her* to change.

I also had a great deal of respect for what was built before I came, so even though they needed help because they weren't reaching their financial goals, I respected what they had accomplished against all odds. I needed to consider how I could enhance what they had done and perhaps improve on it but certainly not throw it all out and start over. That was where my gray hair came in: that was the wise thing to do.

I had eight direct reports when I joined the company (who, by the way, were all women). Typically, when a new CEO comes in, he or she wants to bring in his or her own people. Although DK is a great company, I felt the business wasn't as big as the brand, and in many similar situations a new CEO finds fault and replaces the people who might be responsible for the company not doing what it needs to do.

I had a different point of view. I generally like to love the one I'm with unless there's a reason not to, and so I wasn't focused on replacing people; I was focused on evaluating the team. I tried to understand what they did well and what they did not do well. I spent time with my direct reports, and I found that they were all very strong and very good at what they did and that their direct reports were all excellent in their roles. So what was the problem? They were talented, but it became clear that they were not a team. In short order, I determined that it was not the individuals but a collective lack of discipline and leadership, particularly in terms of procedures, timely decisions, and financial opportunities. In short, rules! And the know-how and the will to enforce them.

If you ask people if they like rules, I believe most will say no. Yet internally, we all need rules and we respect them. Where would our streets be without red lights or stop signs? Business is the same. We need to know when to step on the gas and how to navigate. Leadership and discipline go hand in hand. We learn these concepts as children, and in the workplace rules (or policies or plans or corporate governance) are road maps. They must be established and explained in detail, with the benefits outlined clearly. And they must be strictly enforced.

> **Leadership and discipline go hand in hand.**

That was what I did. I figured I had a better shot at delivering the goals that were set forth by the parent company by working with the people who were already there and who had the experience, the history, and the expertise to move forward. If I could get them to work well together, we could meet our goals. Also, I thought to myself, If I can turn the company around using the same team and I'm the only differentiator, that will make quite a statement about management—my management.

That's basically what happened: here I am eight years into a three-year agreement, with the same management team as when I started. The only difference is that the company hasn't missed a financial goal in the last seven years. Before I came, the management team presented a forecast every year that showed numbers that were financially aggressive, and at the end of that year the numbers missed the goal and were never even close. Then they came back the next year with even higher targets on their sales projections, and at the end of that year they again missed their goal by a wide margin. But after I instituted systems that would enable them to work together better, they never missed a number. They were finally able to deliver the financial results they had forecast.

Meeting the numbers is difficult in any business but always essential. It is especially challenging in the women's fashion business, which is filled with chaos. After all, the apparel business requires us to reinvent ourselves every four months with new product lines and new concepts, and so it stands to reason that there's a tremendous amount of volatility. Nevertheless, I believe that the CEO's job is to manage that chaos, and the only way to do that is to have the right structure, the right organization, the right people, the right rules, and the right disciplines. We had a terrific team of truly talented people, and so the people weren't the problem. We just needed operations in place to help them work together, and that's what I believe I brought to the company.

In fact, during those first few months at DKI, I was reminded of a conversation I had had many years earlier, when I first joined PVH. The patriarch of Phillips Van-Heusen was Seymour Phillips, whose grandfather had founded the business. Seymour was in his late seventies or early eighties at the time, and he was a special man. He had dignity, style, and class: when he walked around the office, everyone wanted to bask in his glow.

One day, Bruce Klatsky and I were in the hallway when Seymour walked by and asked us, "Why are we in this business?" One of us (I don't remember who) said, "We're in this to have the greatest brand in the world." "Nope! Try again." "We want to have the largest market share and dominate this marketplace." Seymour was a little happier with this answer, but he clearly had a lesson to impart. He looked straight at us and said, "You know what, guys? There's only one reason you're in business: *to make money*. Yes, there are many benefits accompanying earning profit, but you're in business to make money, and I suggest you never forget that."

I never did forget it, not while I was at PVH and not when I took over Donna Karan International. DKI had to understand that it needed to make money, and to do that, the company needed to establish and follow certain financial rules. First, when you put a number down on a piece of paper and present it, you own it. You must deliver; you must make it happen. Period. Those numbers have to mean something. You have to believe you can do it, and you have to be able to justify, explain, and support that estimate. Those numbers are you: your future, your credibility.

Second, when you put numbers down on a piece of paper, they have to be monitored very closely. I immediately instituted financial controls at DKI that needed to be in place, including once-a-month financial meetings, and all the division senior managers (i.e., all my direct reports and their direct reports, including the division heads Mary Wang, president DKNY; Carol Kerner, president DK Collection; Carol Sharpe, president DKI Retail; and Cathy Volker, Executive VP of Licensing) were required to be at every meeting. In addition, if we had any new interns working in the company, I wanted them to have the benefit of listening to what went on in those meetings so that they could learn about the financial side of the business.

I think our company should be run more like an investment bank than an apparel company. I think we should always have our eyes on the bottom line while at the same time recognizing that having a strong brand and the right products is what will enable us to meet our financial goals. There is nothing more important than having the right product, at the right time, at the right price, in the right quantity. However, having all those elements in place is critical *not* to make you feel good about your work, *not* to make you look good to the rest of the company, *not* even to have the greatest market share. Instead, it's so your company *can make the most money.*

My first order of business was to build trust, financial trust. Credibility. Performance. The company runs like precision clockwork now, and we haven't sacrificed the product. We are not stagnating. We're not holding back creativity. We're just methodical.

Of course, the financial team, headed by Tisha Kalberer, applauded this attention to discipline, and the employees wanted leadership. Many people had been with the company a long time and wanted to see success and were eagerly waiting for someone to come in and lead. I'm not afraid to stand up for what I think is the right thing to do, and I wasn't going to let anyone stand in my way as I established discipline at DKI. I had the title that enabled me to make changes, but I also knew I was in the right. I knew what LVMH wanted, and that gave me an enormous amount of strength. The major operating principle of LVMH is to support the creative people and give them an environment in which they can thrive. Yet it's a business, and the business has to work. All the CEOs of LVMH are charged with that mandate: to ensure that there is a proper blend of creativity and business. This mandate was spelled out in a letter from Bernard Arnault to our shareholders in a recent annual report.

I had been a corporate officer for 15 years by the time I joined DKI. I knew what LVMH was looking for and what it expected: they had made it quite clear. And I knew how to present to them. Also, as I had told Donna, I was pure of heart. I wasn't there for personal gain. I wasn't there to fight for the CEO job in Paris. I was there to deliver on the plan and thank LVMH for its confidence in me. All I really wanted was a new start, and I was hell-bent on doing the right thing. Couple that with not being needy and with the skills and experience of having led departments, divisions, and an entire company, time and time again, and I believe I was a very effective leader. Trust is the key factor in managing a business from a distance. Paris is a long way from New York. Therefore, I knew we needed to deliver, avoid surprises, partner with the key management in Paris, and build a foundation. We did that.

One thing I thought I was going to teach DKI was how to manage inventory. However, I was surprised to learn that they had a system for managing inventory that was better than any I had ever seen. Inventory is the lifeblood of a company and the death knell of a company. If you have the right product at the right time in the right amount, you're going to have a winning company. If you have the wrong product at the wrong time and too much quantity—more than you need—it destroys a company. Donna Karan International knew how to manage its inventory: that was one of the pleasant surprises.

In contrast, one thing they weren't handling well was shipping. "To fly or not to fly" is one of my favorite business stories. It has to do with air freight from Asia, which may seem mundane but is very "luxurious" in terms of cost. One day, in a management meeting, I wanted to discuss transportation and freight, and I asked a question: "What sea-freight company do you work with, and how has ANERA affected your rates?" Dead silence. I thought maybe they weren't familiar with ANERA—the Asia North America Eastbound Rate Agreement—and so I rephrased the question in simpler terms. Again silence, but this time people were looking around the room uncomfortably, as though they had a secret they didn't want to admit to. I asked, "Am I asking the question wrong?" Sure enough, someone finally said, "We don't ship anything by boat." I was incredulous! *Everybody* in our industry ships by boat, because it costs a fortune to ship by air; it can cost more than 20 times the price of shipping by boat.

When I asked for details, this person said, "We ship everything by air. We really don't have a calendar, so we're always late. As a result, we have to ship by air to ensure that our products arrive on time." Again I couldn't believe what I was hearing, but I calmly asked, "What do you mean you don't have a calendar?" The head of design answered that question: "We have a calendar; we just don't use it." Having a calendar (which is essentially a time and action plan) but not using it is tantamount to not having a calendar. I said, "I don't understand. Do you guys realize the difference in freight between shipping by boat and shipping by air?" They told me they did, "but we need to make decisions at the last minute."

Even though I was committed to learning how the company did things before I made any changes, this was too expensive a problem to ignore. I said to the head of merchandising, "I'm going to give you a week to put together a calendar that has no air freight. Tell me what needs to be done, and we're going to eliminate air freight." She replied respectfully, "We can't do that. It's impossible."

Of course, "it's impossible" is just another way of saying "no," and I wasn't going to take no for an answer, not when so much money in shipping costs was at stake. We were going to find a way to solve this problem. And in this case, it was as simple as setting a calendar and sticking to it.

To make a long story short, they came back with a calendar, and it ended up that if we had, for example, 20 delivery shipments a year, if I allowed them to use air freight for only 2 of those shipments (one in the beginning of fall and one in the beginning of spring), for the other 18 shipments the calendar would enable all of them to ship by boat. This saved the company millions of dollars in that first year.

My point is that even though you want to respect the traditions of a company or a division or a department, you don't just give up when people say things like "This is the way we've always done it" or "There's no other way to do this." There's no way in the world I'm going to accept someone telling me "No, we can't do that" or "We've never done it that way before." And you shouldn't either, even if you're new to the company. Don't accept no for an answer if you think there's a better, more efficient, or less expensive way to do things. I believe it's important for everyone in business today to confront "no" and find a way to turn it into "yes."

29

Licensing Is a Double-Edged Sword

One of my first orders of business was to meet all the people in the company, visit many of the stores where we sold our products, and get a firsthand look at our warehouse and our off-site facilities. My next order of business was our company's licensing partners: we had a diverse group. In particular, I wanted to visit our intimate apparel partner.

I had done considerable research on the brand, and that included looking at all the licensed products. When I went into Macy's, I discovered that its DKNY intimate apparel shop was about the size of a car. Not only was it tiny, it had this weird city skyline in pink, which I thought was in absolutely horrible taste. (Remember, this is what I was avoiding discussing when I first interviewed with Donna. Time for action!) But worse than both the small size and the hideous decor was the shadow thrown over our shop by our competitors, which blotted out DKNY like an eclipse of the sun. With our goals to build this brand, this could not stand.

The presentation really bothered me, because the way a brand is presented at retail often sets the tone for the way it is perceived by consumers. There are really only two ways a brand is perceived at retail: one is by presentation, and the other is by the product itself. One without the other doesn't work.

> There are really only two ways a brand is perceived at retail: one is by presentation, and the other is by the product itself. One without the other doesn't work.

Unfortunately, this wasn't something we could control directly: that space was managed by the company we "licensed" the DKNY name to for intimate apparel. It had a sizable business with DK and DKNY—multiple millions of dollars in this category—and so I asked for a meeting to be set up between our licensing team and the president of the intimate apparel company.

Before the meeting, I studied our licensee, and I learned we were collecting, let's say, a couple of million dollars for advertising per contract. A million dollars sounds like quite a bit of money, and it is. But in the world of advertising, it is not. The cost of a photo shoot alone can be from $250,000 to as much as $500,000. World-class photographers, models, production crews, props, locations, and travel are just some of the costs. Considering the quality of our ad shoots, $1 million does not leave much for the cost of ads in a magazine.

I've said before that the number one rule of advertising is that it needs to break through the clutter because people are obviously bombarded with ads from so many companies every minute of the day, every day. Nevertheless, I'm confident that ads for intimate apparel do break through the clutter and get seen. If you're flipping through a magazine and turn the page and find a good-looking model—male or female—in skimpy underwear, you're going to notice that ad.

However, as much as I appreciated that advertising works in this product category, I thought it was far more important that we consider the fact that our shop presentations weren't good, weren't competitive, were dated, and needed to change. When I met with the president of this licensee, one of the issues I wanted to discuss was our in-store presentation. He did not have a contractual obligation to upgrade the shops or develop new ones, and he told me he was satisfied with the way we looked at retail. As I recall, he said it was "pretty good." I wasn't happy to hear this, because pretty good isn't good enough for me. My licensee, unfortunately, wasn't concerned with brand building, as I was. After earnings, the building of a brand is paramount. In fact, the opposite is true. The truth is that if you make the brand strong, the profits will come.

I proposed that *we* pay to refurbish and renovate our shops: "We're spending a few million a year on advertising, which really doesn't go very far: after production costs, you're getting a few insertions in magazines and a billboard here and there. It's not enough to make a significant change in our business model. So I'd like you to consider taking that advertising money and using it to build shops." I didn't even get to finish my sentence before he said no. I looked at him and said, "I think I made a compelling case to you. You ought to consider it." He said, "No, I need my advertising." I again tried to persuade him: "You're not really advertising all that much. I know it makes you feel good, but it's not making customers buy our product." Again he said, "No, I can't do that." I said I wasn't asking him to pay us the money; I was asking him to help his presentation at retail.

Our meeting ended five minutes later. I walked out and said to the executive VP of licensing, Cathy Volker, and the VP of licensing, Jennifer Morris, "I want out of this license. Find us a new partner." In my opinion, our licensee and DKI were not aligned, and I thought this particular licensing company was thinking on too small a scale, at least with respect to our brand. I think that's an important lesson: a licensee or partner should help move a brand along or improve its performance. But he clearly and emphatically didn't want to do that: those no's were loud and clear.

Of course, we didn't terminate our agreement immediately; there were interim steps and many conversations in which I reiterated how strongly I felt about our goals for our brands. When you realize you're no longer aligned with your partner, it's time to change partners. I want to emphasize that this licensee had an outstanding company with a sizable business, but we finally agreed to part amicably.

We started hunting for a new licensee, and we ended up signing two. The first was Maidenform, a public company that admired our international distribution and wanted to add the prestigious Donna Karan and DKNY brand to its portfolio like the star on top of a Christmas tree. Maidenform agreed to rebuild beautiful new shops: its managers were willing to do much more than our previous licensee, and they were investing with us in doing what we felt needed to be done to build the brand. Sure enough, they doubled the size of our intimate apparel business.

> When you realize you're no longer aligned with your partner, it's time to change partners.

Then we found a licensee for sleepwear, Komar, introduced to us by Gene and Jassin Consulting, and that company also quadrupled the size of our sleepwear business. In about a year, we found two new partners who were more in line with our vision of the brand than the previous licensee, who obviously wasn't. In brand building—and in business in general—when you select partners, it is extraordinarily important to find partners who believe in your vision and share your goals. The lesson is that licensing is a double-edged sword: on the blunt edge, you're lending your name risk-free to a third party who pays you handsomely and takes all the risk: expenses, inventory, and all the business challenges. That's the blunt edge. On the sharp side, the licensee does not own the brand, and at some key times licensees make expedient decisions or decisions that help them financially but are not best for the brand. As the owner of the brand, you must know how to wield the sword.

30

My Favorite
Word Is "No"

On the TV show *Inside the Actors Studio,* the interviewer James Lipton is famous for asking people, "What is your favorite word?" My favorite word is "no" because it opens every door. It makes you think and find new ways of looking at a situation and develop other possible solutions to a problem. As far as I'm concerned, when people say no to me, that forces me to be creative. That's the most exciting challenge in the world: to come up with new ways of doing things and think about how to overcome seemingly insurmountable issues. I've often said, "Behind anyone with vision, there are 50 well-intentioned people undermining that vision."

Here's an example that resulted in revolutionary advertising and marketing of the DKNY brand. Several years ago I was flipping through channels on TV, and I got to the Yankees station. I stopped for a minute to watch, and I noticed there was an orange billboard with Japanese characters behind Hideki Matsui, who was playing right field. At that moment, the batter hit a home run into the stands, over Matsui's head. The camera zoomed in, and the entire TV screen was filled with the Japanese characters. That's all I saw: the billboard with the logo of the company that had advertised there. I thought to myself, What an amazing piece of advertising!

That image stayed with me because I had been looking for a dramatic place to advertise ever since we lost space on our Soho wall, one of

> My favorite word is "no" because it opens every door. It makes you think and find new ways of looking at a situation and develop other possible solutions to a problem.

the last painted billboards in Manhattan. It was two stories high and was painted with a giant DKNY logo that featured the Statue of Liberty and New York City skyscrapers inside the letters. It was our very famous visual for the brand. There was no mention of our products, no address, no other information: just the letters, which made a huge statement. In fact, it became such an iconic billboard that many TV shows and movies that filmed in New York flashed by it because it epitomized the city.

Then, after 16 years (and not long after I started at DKI), the building was sold. We never owned the building; we had simply been leasing space for this wonderful billboard. The company that bought the building was Hollister, owned by Abercrombie & Fitch, and naturally they wanted to paint their own advertisements on it, and they told us ours would be painted over. We tried to negotiate, but there was no way.

Then New York City had something to say: it didn't want to give approval to Abercrombie & Fitch to take down the DKNY sign because some people argued that it was a city landmark. After a year of negotiations on that point, it was decided that the building's owners had the right to do what they wanted with the building, and our letters came down. Our Soho wall was gone.

Since then I had been looking for iconic places to put our logo and different ways to get it out there. When I saw this huge logo at Yankee stadium fill my entire TV screen, I thought, That's it. An iconic brand like the New York Yankees and an iconic brand like DKNY: that's a perfect match! A start to graffitiing our logo in New York City.

Back in the office, I met with our advertising and marketing team to broach this idea. I didn't know how many women go to Yankee Stadium or watch the Yankees on TV, and I knew I would need to justify the idea. Even without women fans, I still believed this idea was worthwhile, because we also had a men's business. I decided that if we had to overspend to get this billboard in Yankee Stadium, I would do that on the basis of the men's business. I've never forgotten a needlework sampler I saw behind one CEO's desk: "Building a brand without advertising is like kissing a girl in the dark: *you* know what you're doing, but no one else does."

I knew what I was doing by suggesting that we put our logo in Yankee Stadium, but as soon as I brought up the idea, everyone in marketing was opposed to it: "We don't have enough money." "If we're going to spend money, we should be spending it on our women's wear, not in Yankee Stadium." "There's no connection for us with the Yankees."

"This is not the brand we should be aligning with." "There aren't enough women fans." I heard a million reasons why we shouldn't do it.

Nevertheless, I still thought advertising in Yankee Stadium was good for the brand, and I believed we would find out that women did go to Yankees games. Then I realized that if I couldn't build consensus with the marketing team, maybe I could build consensus with the operating division, namely, DKNY, DKNY International, and others. But they also fought me on this idea.

Finally, I decided this was one of those times when I just had to be the CEO. I decided, regardless of the cost or their opinions, that we were going to do it. This is what I told the marketing team: "We're going to do this, and I want you to call the Yankees." They reluctantly agreed. When I made that decision, I thought of another needlework sampler, one that was behind the desk of Robert Solomon, one of my early mentors from Van Heusen, which said, "Yea, though I walk through the valley of the shadow of death, I fear no evil, because I'm the meanest son of a b*tch in the valley." That was his way of saying "I have to make tough decisions, and I will."

A week went by, and nobody had called the Yankees. I told them, "Call the New York Yankees or I will." Shortly thereafter, we met with Michael Tusiani, senior vice president, marketing, and Bryan Calka, sales VP, from the Yankees to talk about putting up a billboard in center field at Yankee Stadium. During the course of that conversation, we learned several interesting things: first, we were the only apparel or luxury brand to be in Yankee Stadium. Second, more than 40 percent of the people visiting the stadium were women. Third, a significant portion of their audience consisted of international tourists, who are extremely important to DKNY. My position was supported—although it didn't matter, as I had already decided to advertise in Yankee Stadium. We negotiated to have the DKNY brand shown in an exclusive spot in center field.

Interestingly, since we started the Yankee campaign, the people who argued the most against our sign have been the most fanatical supporters. We've received a lot of goodwill and media attention because the Yankees made the playoffs and won the World Series in 2009, which obviously increased our advertising exposure as well both in the stadium and on TV. In addition, the New York Yankees organization is one of the classiest professional organizations we've ever met. We've participated in charity events, which made us feel good, and shopping events that drove sales and made us feel clever. And 81 nights or days per year, you can turn on the TV and see our iconic brand in iconic Yankee Stadium. And 81 times per season, 50,000-plus fans see our brand in a wonderful light. The idea of bringing two New York icons together is one of those simple decisions that everyone fought against but that turned out to be one of the great marketing moves we've made for the brand.

Please tell me no: it motivates me!

I didn't stop there. I kept looking for ways to brand our company that had never been done before. I was always looking for iconic ways to do it, and I still am. Because we now had sports connections, we were on the radar screen of sports marketing companies. We received a call from Madison Square Garden asking if we would like to advertise at New York Rangers games. We agreed to meet. We found out that the Rangers had lost a key sponsor. Wait until you hear this opportunity: we became the first ever apparel brand to put our name in center ice in a hockey arena, and not just any arena but in New York's Madison Square Garden! We managed to put our iconic brand with another iconic brand, the New York Rangers.

However, absolutely no one in our marketing department, or the company for that matter, wanted to do such a deal, and this was *after* the success we'd had with the New York Yankees. Again they argued, "It's too expensive: we have only so much money to spend, and that's not the best use of our marketing and advertising budget." "It doesn't make sense for us: we don't know how to appeal to hockey people." "Our customers are not hockey fans." "No one will see our logo in the ice." Naturally, with all those "no"s, I became even more interested.

Again, as the CEO, I simply made the decision that we were going to do this. I personally negotiated the terms for our brand to be in the center ice at Madison Square Garden. We were the first apparel brand to appear there: I negotiated an enviable deal, and we were there for two years, right next to Chase Manhattan Bank. Some people thought I did this because I was a hockey fan, but I had never been to a hockey game, let alone a Rangers game. However, watching our brand being seen on TV a million times during a game made me smile 2 million times. It happened because people told me NO! I knew that when you're building brands, you have to find your customers where they are.

We issued a press release that we were going to be the first fashion brand on the ice at MSG. We got excellent press. For two seasons, everyone in New York who went to Rangers games, everyone who watched them on TV, and hockey fans all over the country saw our logo when the games were televised. By the way, the Rangers made it into the National League playoffs those years, which gave us even more exposure. Every time the Rangers skated over the ice, people saw the DKNY logo. That created awareness for the brand, put our name in an unexpected place, and built goodwill. Plus, after everyone said no to this idea, many people in the company came out of the woodwork wanting to go to the games, because so many of their husbands, sons, fathers, and grandfathers followed the Rangers, and so this decision built goodwill within the company (managing to different constituents)—after everyone had said no to the idea.

Here's another example of overcoming NO! We had been working on reenergizing the DKNY logo and looking for exciting new ways to feature it. We were developing new products as well as new marketing and advertising ideas. It was a companywide initiative. About a year ago, our advertising agency came up with a very intriguing concept for the spring advertising campaign. They proposed creating a freestanding pop-up store in a cube that would feature the DKNY logo on all four sides (in other words, completely wrapped in our advertising). We would place these cubes in strategic locations and actually sell products from the cubes. I was fascinated by this combination of advertising and selling, especially in a temporary space that we could move. I thought the idea was incredibly insightful, and so I decided that we should build a series of cubes and install them throughout New York City, especially in places tourists go.

Right away, I got pushback. "There's nowhere in New York that will let us do that." "The city will not give you zoning for freestanding advertising." "There's no location that would work for us." I suggested, "Let's go to a gas station. Let's go to an outside parking lot. Let's go to the South Street Seaport. Let's go to the Water Club, the restaurant on Manhattan's East River, which has terrific views. Let's go to the heliport. Let's go anyplace else outside. Let's go to Times Square and ask if we can put a cube up there, even if it's just a cube, not a store. Let's find out what we *can* do."

Again people fought and said we couldn't do it, and again I refused to take no for an answer. I told them, "Bring in the advertising people: I want to talk directly to whoever is working on this." Our outside advertising production team explained why there was no way they could get this done, giving me 12 different reasons why the city wouldn't do it.

Again I said to everyone, "This wasn't my idea, but I don't care who has the next great idea. I want to do this. Our letters deserve the right to be standing somewhere. What *can* we do?" The team came back to me and suggested building letters and putting them as backdrops in our advertising. I said, "Now you're talking. Let's build the letters and put them on the street. If we can't do the cube, we should be able to do that."

Lo and behold, once the team—led by Patti Cohen, Jackie Bouza, and DKNY's PR expert, Aliza Licht—started to research that idea, they had another idea: to find influential artists and use the DKNY letters and logo as their canvas—in effect, to create new DKNY art. After all, visual artists usually have a cult following, and this would be a nice blend of art and advertising. That was what happened, and there was more. We created a program called DKNY Artworks. Once our creative team got creative, they started to look at the world as our canvas. Then they got excited. The idea blossomed into involving global artists from their respective cities. We first found the funding: this was groundbreaking. Then we selected 10 of the most important cities for our consumers and our business around the world: New York, London, Milan, Paris, Dubai, Kuwait, Hong Kong, Shanghai, Seoul, and Tokyo. Each city had an Artworks program with local artists whom we commissioned to design the billboards and letters for charity. The art was on display for six months and was seen by millions and millions of people. It also received critical acclaim, and at the end of the six months the art was auctioned off.

The moral of this story is that you can't take no for an answer. You have to persevere. There are a dozen reasons why people may say no. It's human nature to say no. It's easier to say no than to find a way to make something happen. "No" is about opportunity, and it's my favorite word. The reason doesn't matter. What's important is that you need to have the stamina, willpower, and drive to persuade people and fight for what you know is the right thing to do. In this case, ultimately, our marketing team executed brilliantly to make this campaign happen. It's important to remember that this was not my idea. The idea came from Laird & Partners, from Trey Laird and particularly Hans Dorsinville, our great collaborators who represent our advertising agency. I refused to let it die or to accept that it couldn't be done. Our marketing and PR team brilliantly executed a worldwide breakthrough campaign. What I'll take credit for is "no," my favorite word, which made this happen. All I can say is how proud we all were of these initiatives.

31

Working with Celebrities

The relationship between celebrities and fashion has been a symbiotic and longstanding one. Thousands of years ago, kings and queens were the celebrities of their day, and their sense of fashion, hairstyles, shoes, and everything else set the tone for their world in their time. More recently, the very idea of celebrity has changed drastically with the advent of reality TV, the blog world, YouTube, and so many other media-creating modern-day forms of communication.

One of the most powerful platforms for celebrities and fashion and a place where the two worlds cling to each other is the world of the red carpet. The way celebrities package and present themselves on the red carpet can define their place in history, pop culture, and fashion; at times, they can even create trends that boom globally overnight. This is true of any red carpet: the Academy Awards (the jewel in the crown), Screen Actors' Guild, Golden Globes, Tonys, and Emmys; the Grammys and other music awards shows; Blockbuster, MTV, People's Choice, movie premieres, our own events, and any other program that is widely seen and talked about.

Especially in today's fast-paced, real-time, info-overloaded society, every step a celebrity makes is tracked, photographed, followed, liked, and of course imitated. Through social media, people have immediate access to see who wore what and can just as immediately comment or pass along other people's opinions. That makes the impact of a certain look, dress, shoe, or hairstyle instant and explosive. But as quickly as a photo appears, it disappears—on to the next thing! That creates a specific challenge for brands—especially fashion brands—to stay relevant in pop-culture discussions. Everyone has to do something different, be the right "it" girl of the moment, and create moments with celebrities that stand out. And then do it over and over again.

Celebrities are one of the best vehicles for out-of-home advertising. They are living, breathing, widely seen, and respected billboards that will be photographed, talked about, and analyzed in terms of the brand, the dress, and the look that they are wearing. The connection and impact of a celebrity are undeniable. When a celebrity wears something new, that can be the moment that launches the entire career of a designer. There is no secret to the massive amounts of free clothing celebrities receive in the hope that they will be photographed wearing the item or even showing it off somehow within their social media universe.

Advertising campaigns use celebrities and not just models for a very specific reason: to align with the "aura" of a specific man or woman. Celebrities don't always have to be A-list Hollywood actors or actresses; they can also be athletes or politicians. Sometimes the most unexpected relationships that are created on the glossy pages of a fashion magazine between a fashion brand and a celebrity are the ones that have had the most impact. The power of celebrity and the right partnerships and alignments can be extremely powerful, whether it is fashion or any other category.

As a fashion brand and company, you have to consider who you are partnering with and analyze that relationship from various angles: their other partnerships, them as a brand and what they are known for, their look and style, their personal life, and the way scandals can affect your direct relationship with them. We have seen many occasions in which a brand has been forced to drop a celebrity partnership because of the scandals in that person's personal life, and sometimes the scandal can elevate the brand as a result of the risk and danger associated with the celebrity. It's an interesting relationship and one that is most certainly mutually beneficial.

Because movies, music, and fashion are a very powerful triumvirate, if we can persuade a celebrity or famous person to wear one of our designs, that can have a tremendous impact not only on publicity but on sales. Men are important but nowhere near as important in terms of their impact as celebrity women when they wear designer fashions.

Those images are high-profile: they're like the shot heard around the world, because the instant a celebrity on the red carpet says she's wearing your dress or if the press reports that she is wearing your dress, that information goes online all over the world, and millions of impressions are made—on TV, in newspapers, in magazines, and on all forms of social media. Consumers see your brand on high-profile beautiful people. Celebrities enhance your brand, and they can bring excitement, energy, goodwill, and endorsement of your design ethic. The next day, newspapers across the country and around the world show these women wearing your dresses. After that come the weekly magazines and then the monthlies, and that publicity can continue for a long, long time even though the original image may be long gone.

I would go so far as to say that one dress can change the direction of a company because it brings such incredible exposure over a relatively short period. Everything is so instantaneous today and there's such an amazing interest in fashion that a dress can be seen around the world overnight: people in China will walk into a store the day after an awards ceremony, knowing you dressed Rita Ora or Taylor Swift the night before. As a result, the value of that publicity and that celebrity endorsing your product by wearing it is incalculable. Because of that, there is a tremendous amount of competition and effort to dress celebrities.

Here are just a few of the famous women who have worn Donna Karan fashions during my tenure: Jennifer Aniston, Kate Beckinsale, Beyoncé, Emilia Clarke, Penélope Cruz, Cara Delevingne, Nina Dobrev, Megan Fox, Gina Gershon, Greta Gerwig, Ashley Greene, Anna Gunn, Naomie Harris, Iman, Kim Kardashian, Anna Kendrick, Karlie Kloss, Heidi Klum, Diane Kruger, Ali Larter, Jennifer Lopez, Camila Alves McConaughey, Rose McGowan, Debra Messing, Elisabeth Moss, Rita Ora, Gwyneth Paltrow, Hilary Rhoda, Rihanna, Emmy Rossum, Susan Sarandon, Hailee Steinfeld, Barbra Streisand, Taylor Swift, Sofía Vergara, Kerry Washington, Allison Williams. That's an impressive list.

The power of Hollywood, TV, and the music world is extraordinary: in fact, I believe someone from the music industry can have even more of an impact than someone from Hollywood, because people listen to music every day. That's just my opinion, however; either way, celebrity dressing is an important part of marketing our fashions. Personally, I was most excited when Taylor Swift wore us to the 2013 Golden Globes, and she looked beautiful.

Weber's World

32

We Are in the Want Business

When I joined DKI and LVMH, I entered a new world that was global in scope: fashion, women's designer fashion—all bigger than life. Sometimes you have to put business in perspective. Pretty much anyone I am addressing in this book *needs* nothing. If each and every one of you lives to be 100 years old, you already have all the clothes, shoes, or handbags you will ever need. Yet our industry sells billions of dollars per year of ideas because people *want* something new. It's our job to *create* that want! To achieve this, we develop new fashions. Every year we are charged with creating something new: we develop new products in new silhouettes, new colors, and new styles.

We create things that you don't need but really, really want. Dresses in every fabric, color, and style you can think of and in every fit, from loose-fitting to skintight. In men's suits, there are now three fits available: classic fit, (democratic fit, which is suitable for many people), slim fit, and superslim. Yesterday, a guy was happy in his classic-fit suit; today, most men are putting their classic suits aside and retrofitting a new wardrobe to slim fit.

Women's shoes are my favorite, and women spend a lot of time and (thankfully) disposable income on flats, sneakers, wedge sneakers, two-inch heels, and spiked four-inch heels. And they are all "in style." We have trained the consumer to have wardrobes for every occasion. Ka-ching! That's the fashion business, creating the want. We create your need to look good, to feel good, to fit in or stand out, to blend in or make a statement—a fashion statement. It's all about the product.

The difference between need and want is fascinating to me. In our business, I think you have to recognize that no one needs what you're offering, but they do want it. How do we make them want it? Our whole industry—including fashion, retail, and luxury goods—is predicated on persuading you to change your mind: we make whatever you thought you were comfortable in less relevant, and then we influence you to put it aside and go buy something else, something new. The entire world of advertising and marketing is also a coconspirator in persuading you to buy things you don't need but want and convincing you that one company's products are better than those of its competitors.

> That's the fashion business, creating the want. We create your need to look good, to feel good, to fit in or stand out, to blend in or make a statement—a fashion statement.

Since we're selling something that no one needs, we have to make people want our products. That entails a tremendous responsibility and burden to create things that are different, new, and fresh through color, style, fit, or even technology.

Developing new ideas is what drives our business. If you are in this business, you need to recognize that your company or products need to always strive to be something different. That's the essence of the fashion business. Don't kid yourself: it's all about creating things people don't need. If you understand that, you can be very successful in this business.

33

It's All About Fashion

The fashion business is always and forever all about *the product*. You can have the best brand name, the best designer, the best advertising, the best salespeople, and the best price, but it's all for nothing if the product is not right. Donna Karan would say it's about the body, the mind, and the soul. She doesn't just dress the body; she addresses the mind.

I take it further. I have always admired and respected the role that apparel plays in society. We are an industry that employs millions of people throughout the world. Most third world countries' early infrastructures begin with manufacturing apparel. It's labor-intensive, the skills are easily taught, and the labor prices are attractive for global importing and commerce. Simply put, the industry supplies jobs and provides hope and opportunity. But it's always about the product.

In the hierarchy of needs, the need for shelter and warmth comes first. That translates into a place to live. Clothing provides protection: it can be utilitarian, but clothing and accessories are also important to the psyche. Our products help build self-esteem, and the resulting confidence changes people's lives for the better.

I have never heard anyone say he or she doesn't want to look good. Billions of dollars are spent every year on improving the way people look, or helping them to *think* they look good. Feeling and looking good is essential to finding your soul mate. It promotes the procreation of the species. The right look helps you find a job, integrate with your peers, and make friends and promotes acceptance by other individuals. In many respects, clothing is one of the five essentials, right after shelter, food, water, and air. Clothing is necessary to sustain life. The next time you see a guy in a cool suit, think what signals it is sending and their rightful importance. The next time you see a woman in incredible shoes, think about the statement she is making. What impact does she have on those around her? Also, think about who was provided the work to manufacture those clothes or shoes, whether in Italy, Brazil, or China. Think about all the families that were supported and all the children being educated because of his suit or her shoes. It's all about the product.

> You can run from product, but you can't hide: sooner or later you need to know your product offerings. What is working, and what is not?

I have worked with great designers—both Calvin Klein and Donna Karan—and hundreds of other designers and support staff. The great ones see it and know great from "stuff." If you can't see the difference, you should find a different career or recognize that many others get it and that their prospect for success may be better than yours. Admittedly, there are rewarding careers in fashion that are not product-related, but sooner or later product comes into play.

There are CEOs in our business—very successful CEOs, I might add—whose expertise lies in finance, administration, or sales. You can run from product, but you can't hide: sooner or later you need to know your product offerings. What is working, and what is not? You will be making financial commitments and betting or risking the franchise on the decisions surrounding your products. Therefore, you need to understand what makes a good product. You certainly need to appreciate that. Some of the finest financial people I have worked with have developed a keen sense of product. In contrast, I have heard many executives say, Don't ask me; I haven't a clue what works. But they do.

If you're a comedienne, learn jokes; if you are a pilot, fly planes. If you're a luxury executive, learn product. And know how to eliminate boring in favor of the awe-inspiring. Success is all about the product.

34

On a Scale of
1 to 10 . . .

Over the course of my career, I've worked with designers who are awe-inspiring. When I'm in a showroom looking at a collection, my jaw literally drops. I realize now how smart I was *not* staying in design, because when I look at this collection and consider the thought process that went into it, I'm always impressed by how gifted and talented our designers are. I find myself wondering, Where do these colors come from? How did they think of doing this? How do they know how to fit a woman this way? It's unbelievable, and I'm always awestruck, and when I feel that way, I really appreciate the opportunity to be part of the fashion industry.

In contrast, I've worked with designers who showed me their designs for sign-off, and I just didn't think they were compelling. I sat in our showrooms and watched the models walk in. They were all beautiful girls, six feet tall and slender, and the clothes fit them perfectly. Their job was to make those products look even better than what the designers had designed. But the merchandise—our products—didn't have what was needed to stand out. They didn't break through the clutter. I call it stuff; some people call it filler. If we needed a product line with 10 styles, one or two of them were great, but the rest were just clutter, filling the space. How do you tell people that?

I have always been in a position to critique or decide on product content. Being honest and direct with people about their work is very difficult. Most people work hard to develop products they think are good, and that makes it even harder to tell them nicely that their work isn't good after all. The key word there is "nicely," because it's easy to be brutal but it's not easy to be gentle. I believe senior executives should have sensitivity to this, some humility. Unfortunately, there are too many who are arrogant or mean or just don't have the social graces to give criticism politely.

I have found that the best way is to use a rating system, since it's a straightforward concept that everyone is familiar with. For example, movies, restaurants, and hotels are all rated by the star system: one star means it's terrible, four stars means it's amazing. I decided to use a rating system of 1 to 10, and I've found it to be very effective.

I can usually tell within 15 seconds where something, or an entire collection, falls on my 1–10 rating system. Fortunately, I'm at a level where I'm working with people who have thick enough skin that I can usually say to them, "That over there is a 6, and we're not in the business of 6s. We have to replace it with something else." You can't be mediocre and be successful in this business.

I've also worked with people who are adamant that their work is a 10, and that makes the review process much more difficult and awkward. I've been in product meetings in which there are three designers in a room, two merchants, someone from marketing, and others. We needed to review the designs, and we were looking at a line of 12 dresses in which only 3 were really spectacular, 3 others made the models look frumpy, and the colors of 3 others were just awful. In fact, I was disappointed that this was what the designers had brought us. But critiquing someone's work when there are so many people in the room is even more difficult than when it's one on one. In situations like that, I still used my 1–10 rating system, but I asked everyone in the room to rate each design anonymously by writing down a number from 1 to 10 on a piece of paper, which they then folded and put in a hat.

You'd be surprised at how people rank things when they can do so anonymously and don't have to look someone in the eye and tell that person they don't like it. This system was simple but effective: I'd have 10 people in the room, and when I opened all the slips of paper, sure enough, 6 of the people had ranked it a 4 or a 5 rather than a 10. When that happens, there's no more discussion; the review is over, and it's easier for the designers to accept the decision because it's not as personal. It allows the person who is doing the critique to be honest without the awkwardness of having to tell someone to his or her face.

It's difficult to tell people that their work isn't good, but it's even worse when they don't know it themselves. I believe that when people present to me, they should be showing me a line of 10s. They should be sending only their best work. I think you need to self-edit and self-critique before you present to anyone in management. That's a big lesson: if it isn't great, don't even show it. If you need more time, ask for more time; that's better than showing product that isn't great and that you yourself are not satisfied with. This applies to designs, advertising photos or layouts, presentations, and anything that needs to be displayed, After all, if you don't think it's a 10, why should anyone else?

There is no substitute for good taste. I never compromise on taste level. Products are either right or wrong, good or bad, sexy or not. They either move us or they don't. I look for awe-inspiring; the rest is stuff. I want products that must be recognized as great (or at least appreciated). To make it in this business, you need to know the difference between chicken salad and chicken s#+t!

The worst-case scenario is when someone argues that his or work is great when it clearly isn't. On a number of occasions, we unfortunately hired a new designer who had a terrific reputation. Yet the first line that designer presented to me was so bad, I couldn't believe what I was looking at. Then, when I started to ask about the designs and inform the designer that in my view they were 3s, 4s, and 5s, the designer tried to debate with me, saying they were 7s, 8s, and 9s. At that point I left the room: I wasn't going to debate good taste.

> There is no substitute for good taste. I never compromise on taste level. Products are either right or wrong, good or bad, sexy or not.

Those designers were no longer with our company after a week or a month, let go because I firmly believe you can't compromise on taste and you shouldn't have to discuss it. You can discuss different points of view, but you should never have to discuss whether product is impactful, tasteful, or just right.

Frankly, if you can't tell that, you have no business being in a design or creative role. When you get ready each day and look in the mirror, you know when you look great—your hair is perfect, and what you're wearing is stylish and well put together—and you know when you don't, maybe because something doesn't fit right or for a dozen other reasons. You need to learn the difference between good and bad, and you need to be able to see it. If you don't, you won't be successful in design or in business in general, because everything in business is part art and part science.

Personally, I agree with Oscar Wilde, who said, "I have the simplest tastes: I am always satisfied with the best." I've added my own spin: there's no substitute for good taste. If you don't know the difference between good and great, you don't belong in the fashion business. I don't care who you are. I've often said to people, When I ask you for an opinion, I already have it. I really only need my own. You need to develop that same sense and skill. Donna Karan International, both the collection and DKNY, have incredible taste. The products are all exceptional. When we are right, we're very right. When we're wrong, we manage. But in this company there is no compromise on taste.

35

The World
Series Versus
the World Cup

T he makers of designer brands and luxury brands are not thinking only about finding one or two channels of distribution in
the United States. They're thinking, How I can expand globally,
and what do I need to do to get there? To this day, there are still very
large American companies whose products are earmarked for sale
only in North America, and they can make a living doing that. Donna
Karan International has been a global brand since it started in 1991.
One of the original partners was of Japanese origin, and he obviously
understood the world. Of course, LVMH was always a global company too, because it's rooted in the tradition of European companies
that didn't have the huge American market and therefore had to look
outside their borders even before there was a European Union. As a
result, European companies adapted early to the demands of doing
business internationally and shipped products and built stores all over
the world, whereas most American companies took a while to catch on
to the fact that the world is their marketplace.

Many American companies delayed going global because the
United States has such a huge marketplace right here at home.
However, the size of our market is both a blessing and a curse. It's a
blessing because we can sell so much product domestically. It's a
curse because we didn't need to learn how to sell internationally and
as a result were very late in figuring it out. For example, the first time
General Motors tried to sell automobiles in Japan, it built cars with the
steering wheel on the left side, just as it is here in the United States.

However, the Japanese drive on the right side. And GM wondered why it wasn't successful in the Japan market.

The United States may have a great impact on the world, but we're still only a small part of it. I learned that when PVH bought Gant, which was very successful internationally and very weak in the United States. We were running the U.S. part, and our licensed partner consisted of three guys based in Sweden: two designers and an operating guy who had built a brilliantly profitable company that they were running internationally. Because we owned the Gant trademark, the Swedish licensee had to answer to us, and one day when the CEO of the Swedish company and I were having a difference of opinion, he said to me, "You Americans think the World Series is a baseball game played in Yankee Stadium. The rest of the world realizes the World Series is the World Cup playing football [soccer] in every country of the world." That was his way of telling us, Wake up, guys: there's more to the world than just the United States.

When you think about products and style and fashion, you have to develop a content or a line or a plan that considers *all* markets. In fact, there may be significant differences even within a single country, especially one as large and diverse as the United States. For example, the product concept or line for one geographic region could be very basic, whereas in another area of the United States such as New York or Los Angeles it could be very sophisticated. There are also markets in Europe and Asia that prefer more sophisticated designs, for example, Italy and Japan, where people dress very fashionably.

Therefore, when you are developing product and building a business, you have to ask, How can I make this universal? You need to consider how your product line takes into consideration the fact that there is a world out there that goes beyond our borders, and you have to be able to set up a network that provides product for the world.

Also, you need to recognize that every market is different. There are unique differences in every country and there are unique similarities, and when you do business on an international basis, you need to be thinking about this. At the same time, you can't assume that all your customers around the world are going to come to New York: you have to swim where the fish are swimming. For the European markets, you have to be represented in Paris, Milan, or London or all three so that you can reach your Europe-based customers. Many people from Asia or the Middle East also go to Europe because of these marketplaces, and so you have to be set up in those locations with a contact, sales help, and information for those customers.

The opportunities for businesses are global, and so you must think globally and develop a product line that works around the world. Many companies make the mistake of thinking they need different product lines for different regions, and ultimately that hurts them, because we now live and work in an instantaneous global society. What happens in New York today is seen around the world, and what happens in China is seen here. Runway shows are now seen all over the world, and so when customers go to your shop in Beijing or Rome or London, they're expecting to see what they saw on the runway, not some second-class product line. Yet to this day there are people working in our industry who don't understand that and still develop different product lines for different countries. There are sometimes small "capsule" collections or items that can be developed, but product lines must be universal.

> At the same time, you can't assume that all your customers around the world are going to come to New York: you have to swim where the fish are swimming.

Although the product design should be the same the world over, you do need to consider how the fit may differ in various countries, and you may need to expand the sizes. That doesn't mean the size itself changes: a size 2 in Hong Kong should be identical to a size 2 in New York. However, the difference may be in the range of sizes: for example, you might start with a size 00 in Asia, whereas the smallest size in the United States might be a size 2. Also, you may not find sizes 12 or 14 in Hong Kong, whereas you probably will find those sizes in New York and throughout the United States, because Americans are larger than people in many other cultures. Women's clothing in Asia may go up only to a size 8. Yet there are still companies that haven't figured out how to fit their merchandise for the entire world.

If a designer is catering to tourists from around the world, it should offer the full range of sizes. However, I've seen companies that have gone to Asia with a fit that just doesn't make any sense: their sleeves are too long or their hemlines are too long. These are nuances of doing business internationally that you have to learn. First and foremost, when you're building a global brand, it should represent the same thing throughout the world.

Unfortunately, I've worked with partners internationally that tried to persuade my company that we didn't understand their culture's marketing or that we needed a different product line because the one we had wouldn't work in their market. However, consumers are the same all over the world. There are some factors you need to consider when developing a product line that will work internationally: for example, in Asia, some of the blush colors don't work well with people's complexions, and so clothing in those colors won't sell as well as it will elsewhere. But you should have enough product that buyers can purchase from your line offering without your having to make special products for them that don't exist anywhere else.

You also need to think about your pricing when selling globally. For example, many countries have VATs—value-added taxes—on which consumers pay an additional purchasing tax. In some countries, this tax can be as high as 20 percent, and that additional cost can have a significant impact on your pricing structures. For example, if I buy a designer brand men's suit in New York for $1,000, that suit might cost $1,250 in London because of the VAT. As a result, those taxes could push your product mix out of whack with patterns of global travel. You need to decide whether you're going to pass along that additional cost to your customers. In addition, some companies set up their websites so that consumers are not able to see what the same product costs in different countries. For example, if you're living in Hong Kong and you want to see what the price is in New York for the same product, you will probably be barred from the U.S. website.

Finally, even the advertising or editorial is a factor when you're doing business globally. Some companies choose the same thing for every editorial, whether it's *Vogue* in the United States or *Vogue* in Japan or Hong Kong. Then there are other items that are picked up by different geographical regions that would appeal more to their customer base than what we might have here or somewhere else. It's a big world, and our line is designed to encompass it all, recognizing that there are differences in geographic regions. In the Middle East, they're not allowed to show shoulders; they're not allowed to show skin. If we're doing ads, we have to make sure during the photo-shoot process that some of the women are covered up.

Remember, the World Series is not a baseball game in Yankee Stadium: there's more to the world than just the United States.

36

Indefensible

I n business, you're not always going to agree with your coworkers, your staff, or even your superiors. Sometimes you'll win those disagreements, and sometimes you won't. Sometimes you lose even when you're right. You can have whatever point of view you want; it's the way you *express* that viewpoint that matters. You can't get excited or angry or scream at people. You need to recognize that people in business want to see you as someone who understands what the important issues are and who can handle problems while maintaining control. People don't like drama. Even though our business is filled with drama (and yours may be too), the people who know how to manage through the chaos or crises are the ones who are going to have the most success.

I keep in mind something one of the board members at PVH told me when I became CEO: "A CEO is like an eagle flying through a snowstorm: you have to be level and consistent as you navigate through that snowstorm." That's my advice to anyone in business: no matter what issues you face and no matter where you are on your career ladder, you need to keep three things in mind when getting into any discussion that's heated. First, you need to choose your battles carefully: think long and hard before you open your mouth whether what you're concerned about is really worth arguing for. Second, if you're going to argue a point, you need to make sure you are dead right and have all the facts you need to back you up. As I often say, the only argument I ever want to enter is one in which the other person is in an indefensible position. Third, you have to know how to control your emotions.

> You need to choose your battles carefully: think long and hard before you open your mouth whether what you're concerned about is really worth arguing for.

One senior executive I worked with was always losing his cool and getting angry during meetings, and that put everyone at those meetings in a bad or unhappy mood. Even when he was 100 percent right and needed to be forceful in what he was trying to convey because we weren't meeting our financial goals or there had been a major snafu that shouldn't have happened, there was no reason for him to have a temper tantrum. He ended up having to circle back and apologize for his behavior—even though he was right.

> The only argument I ever want to enter is one in which the other person is in an indefensible position.

In contrast, I've worked with executives (and I aim for this myself) who can deliver good news *and* bad news and still leave everyone smiling and knowing what he or she needs to do to improve. Handling yourself that way doesn't mean you need to be a meek, weak, or sweet softy; it means you need to be professional at all times. You should be seen as someone who fixes problems, not affixes blame.

When you're a leader of a company or a division or a department, you have a responsibility to the people you work with. You're setting the tone. You're supposed to respect the office that you hold, but more important, you want the people around you to respect that office. You need to be beyond reproach. I look at it as if you're the president of the United States: you have to be careful in everything you say because everything you say has great import. When you have an important position in a company, the people who work for you need to see you as a leader who has moral standards, who understands the challenges of business, who is that eagle in a snowstorm. No matter what comes your way, you have to be held in the highest regard and set a certain standard.

Moreover, I believe that if you are arguing with somebody and you lose your temper and start yelling or swearing or storm out of the room, you've lost that argument no matter how right you are. If the other person has kept his cool, he's won. I've made it a conscious goal to never swear in the workplace, to never raise my voice, and to never show anger, no matter how upset I am.*

---

*At least I try. I actually announce my cuss words and keep count. In 2013, I used seven "S" curses and three "F" curses. In 2014, it's been a tough year: I already have 10 of each.

I think I've lost my cool twice in my life in business, because I really believe in that responsibility. I know that I am setting a tone and a standard for how everyone else in my company communicates. That applies whether I'm speaking or writing to someone, even (probably especially) when communicating by e-mail. Another quote I've heard is never put anything in writing that you wouldn't want to see on the cover of the *Wall Street Journal.* Anybody could read every e-mail I've ever written at this company and I would be able to sleep at night knowing that there's nothing there that I'd be sorry about writing.

> You should be seen as someone who fixes problems, not affixes blame.

Sometimes your life passes before you: you make a mistake, and you pay a price for it. The reaction could be as simple as someone walking by you and rolling her eyes, or you might hear later that someone thought you behaved inappropriately. Then there are times when you came prepared to a meeting, you knew your subject matter, you presented it calmly and in an organized way, and you can see the positive reaction of your peers and senior people. You're getting firsthand feedback on what's working.

You can find role models for this everywhere. Watch them and learn from them. You're going to see both people you want to emulate and people you never want to be like. Watch what happens when someone loses his cool in a meeting: it doesn't matter what that person is saying—even if he's right—because he just lost the argument. That person—male or female—is not going to be respected no matter what his or her point of view is. Then watch people who handle themselves well. Learn from them and emulate them.

37

Don't Judge a
Book by Its Cover

am a great interviewer—not just good but great. I know how to pick people clean. Regardless of how much someone prepares, that person will end up talking about things he or she never dreamed of or intended to talk about. I know how to size people up, read their minds, and see their characters. I know what's important to them, and then I determine if they can do the job.

Some people believe that creative types such as designers need to look the part. I disagree. Some of the best people I've ever hired in creative design were only five feet tall or 100 pounds overweight or were individuals you wouldn't want to sit next to you at a dinner table, but they were creative geniuses. Therefore, when you're evaluating people, you need to get past how they look and find out whether they have what it takes to succeed in the position for which you're interviewing them.

I begin every interview in the same manner. If you got to sit in front of me; if you made it through the screening; if you were recommended by an associate, friend, family member, former colleague, senior executive, corporate executive, or CEO; or if your résumé caught my attention, you are going to be interviewed seriously.

First and foremost, the law correctly outlines what you can and cannot ask in an interview. Most people know these subjects and questions. They are designed to eliminate bias from the process. If you are senior enough, you may want to share some details of your life to give your interviewer insight into who you are. I, for one, will ask, "Is there anyone in your immediate family who might be employed who would be a competitor of the company you're interviewing with?" Another question I typically ask is, "This position requires travel. Is there any reason you may not be able to travel?" I'm not interested in the details of people's personal lives, but I do need to know if they can fulfill the demands of the job.

I begin every interview with a plan, which I share with the candidate. I explain the interview process along these lines: "First I'm going to tell you something about myself, and then I'm going to tell you something about the company and the position you're interviewing for. Then we're going to talk about you. Afterward, I'll summarize and let you know where you stand." I do this because I want people to know precisely what I thought, what may or may not have resonated well, and, most important, whether they will be considered for the position. Many people are uncomfortable stating the facts and being this direct, but I feel that a candidate wants to know all this.

I like to start by opening up and giving people some insight into me so that they will be comfortable and more inclined to talk about themselves. I've never been a salesman, but I can sell the company with the best of them. Before they talk, I want them to want this job. When I interview people, that means they sufficiently impressed my colleagues who interviewed them before they got to me, and so I take these candidates seriously. They may be great for the company, and so I want them presold on the job for which they're interviewing.

I then ask them whether they have any questions, which I will answer in depth. You learn quite a bit about people from the questions they ask. Then it's my turn to ask questions. My job is to determine if this person would be right for our company. Will he or she be successful in our company? I take hiring as a serious responsibility and a personal burden. If you hire someone who is not working, you may have less responsibility because at least you gave that person a job and some dignity. However, if that person turns out to be wrong for the job, you have wasted his or her time, which could have been used to pursue the correct opportunity, and that person is out of work again.

Hiring someone who is already well positioned and working is a tremendous responsibility if that person fails. Yes, we're all adults, and ultimately that person agreed to take a risk and change jobs, but it is the interviewer's responsibility to outline clearly and succinctly what's expected and to truthfully detail the company and its style. I take this process very seriously. I do not like playing with people's lives. It's a burden I don't like, but it's one I have to accept; therefore, I make it clear to candidates that they should not try to convince me if they are not what they say they are.

There is a series of standard questions I may ask any and all candidates. For specific responsibilities, I ask very specific questions. If you are in U.S. sales, who do you know? What level of executive will return your call? If you are in global sourcing, in what countries are you most comfortable producing? Are there countries whose infrastructure may prohibit you from placing orders?

For example, let's discuss interviewing a creative director or head of design for a fashion company. Keep in mind that I am the president and/or CEO, not the senior creative person in the company. Therefore, as the head of a business unit, I am looking at a candidate as a creator and my questions are couched in that vein. Creative managers have already met these candidates first, and I interview them as a final arbiter.

Here are some of the questions I would ask: Where do you get inspiration? How do you begin to put a collection together? If I said to you that we are an urban brand, city, modern, and we want a collection for day into night, where would you begin? What is the first presentation you would make to management with your ideas? In what format would it be? Where would you find color? How would you determine style? Do you have an idea of what the fit of the product might be? Is there any special trim on the collection? Do you have any new ideas for buttons or labels? What prices do you see the collection selling for? Where do you envision the production being done? Whose design ethos do you admire, and why?

These are a sample of the questions I ask, and each one has follow-up questions designed to engage and challenge the candidate. Each of the follow-ups is aimed at learning the candidate's point of view. Are you a visionary? Can you handle pressure? That's important because this is a pressure business.

For me, the process—the way you work—is most important. If I don't like your methods, I won't hire you. I have seen both men and women cry in interviews. I have heard confessions of doubt; I have seen confidence erode. I have learned a lot from candidates. I interviewed a guy who said he hated women: wrong company, wrong country, wrong century. I've interviewed people whose role was to travel to Asia to negotiate manufacturing agreements but they could not travel because of family responsibilities. In another interview, I discovered that a merchant was color-blind, and this was after the candidate had been interviewed by my other colleagues. Obviously, that discovery made me lose faith in those colleagues who interviewed this candidate before me in the interview process.

Just for good measure, I have questions designed to trick candidates.

My advice: whether you're the interviewer or interviewee, have a plan and be precise. When you're the interviewee, keep in mind that the company needs you more than you need the company. That won't stop them from trying to trip you up. Be confident but don't lie. If you have a discipline you need to learn but are strong in critical areas, a well-run company should provide infrastructure to support you. In the end, a good interviewer is protecting the company and you. If you're the interviewer, be responsible: you're playing with people's lives.

> When you're the interviewee, keep in mind that the company needs you more than you need the company. That won't stop them from trying to trip you up. Be confident but don't lie.

38

Mentoring Talent

As I've become more successful in my career, I've also become more interested in helping others advance in their careers. Remember, I wrote at the beginning of this book that I didn't have any advisors or mentors when I was starting out (though I certainly received a lot of training during my years at PVH, for which I am very appreciative). Therefore, I've made it a point to seek out younger and more junior employees who I believe have potential and have made it my business to mentor them.

I met one of my mentees while I was president of PVH. Our offices were in New York, but our administrative offices and retail group were in Bridgewater, New Jersey. One day the president of the retail group, Michael Zaccaro, asked to have a drink with me. He wanted to hire a young man to be the head of marketing for the retail group at a nice salary and wanted me to meet this candidate before he extended an offer to him, and I did. This candidate, Mike Kelly, was a very interesting guy: he had never gone to college, he had a very varied background in marketing and retail, and he had worked his way up the hard way. He had lots of rough edges, but his style showed through. He also wasn't an East Coaster: he came from Chicago, and so he brought an entirely fresh Midwestern sensibility to his work. When I met him, he was about 40 years old and I was about 50.

During that first meeting, I found him to be a very insightful, charming guy. I liked him. He'd had a nice career, but it was stagnant. We hired him and put him in a cubbyhole in New Jersey, doing in-store retail marketing. But he had a passion for the business, and I could tell from the way he talked that there was something special about him, that he could do more than the work he was doing. And he was smarter than most people with MBAs I had met. I kept an eye on him to see if he could handle greater responsibilities.

As luck would have it, he had just started playing golf and I had started about a year and a half earlier, so we talked a bit about golf. He described all the trials and tribulations he was having, which I had gone through a year and a half earlier, and I suggested that we play together, which we did. Of course, being on a golf course for four hours gave us more time to talk, and the more I got to know him, the more I liked what he had to say. He was doing small in-store photo shoots, but he came up with very clever ideas to make the brands he was involved with more interesting.

His work started to impress me, and whenever we were together on the golf course or anywhere else, I asked him questions about his work. And the more I probed, the more he came back at me with insightful answers and the more I saw that he "got it." I decided this guy deserved a shot at something bigger than what he was doing, and so a few months after we met, I opened an important opportunity for him and the company: I asked Mike to come with me to our next photo shoot, in Miami, to see what he could do on a national advertising campaign. I was committed to elevating our brands and had decided we could do that through the creative arts and through advertising, and this was going to be a major photo shoot.

This was important for him, because the ads we would be shooting in Miami were light-years from the in-store visuals and catalog shoots he had been doing in New Jersey and the stakes were different. Essentially, I asked him to be my assistant art director on the shoot and help with all the preproduction work. Naturally, he jumped at the chance even though he would have to fulfill all his commitments for his regular job while working on this special assignment with me. (This was not unlike what Bruce Klatsky did for me in my first job.)

Preproduction on a photo shoot is very time-consuming. Many people think doing a photo shoot is easy because of what they see on TV: the photographer, the lights, the models, and so forth. However, the preproduction work takes many weeks because you need to decide what clothes you want to photograph, make sure they fit the models, alter the clothes, prepare them for shipment, do all the styling, and make sure you have the proper shoes, socks, pants, shorts, bathing suits, everything. And that was just for Izod, our active brand. For our dress shirts, we needed suits in the right size, and many times people would send a size 40 suit for a model who had a thirty-two-inch waist, but when we got on set, we would realize we needed size 40 long because the models were so tall.

He handled all these preparations and more for just the preproduction work; that was extremely challenging, especially on this scale, because we were photographing a number of brands, first on the beach, then at South Beach bars and on a local golf course. I had experience doing all this because when I was very young, the company had seen something special in me and had trained me and helped me learn what needed to be done in advertising. Now I was mentoring, doing for someone else that which had been done for me years earlier.

Once we got started, I saw that his ideas and his vision and his work were extraordinary. He had a lot to learn, but he had something to offer. He was the perfect complement to me because he thought about things that I didn't. For example, I was focused on the photographer, the models, and which shirts and ties we were going to feature in these ads. Meanwhile, he was thinking about props: since we were shooting the ads on the beach, he suggested that we use surfboards, kayaks, even parachutes for parasailing, and many other props that I had never thought about using. I was solely focused on the concept, which was to show men's dress shirts in places you wouldn't typically see them, such as a guy coming out of the water wearing a shirt and tie.

Instead, following his idea, we set up four brightly colored surfboards and dressed the models in bathing suits, with bright-colored shirt-and-tie combinations in front of the surfboards. We shot pictures like nothing anyone had ever seen before. We set up tents and hammocks and shot underwater, and he had something to add to every idea. The work we did was incredible, and as a result, this first photo shoot helped us bond—and led to many more opportunities and many more photo shoots for us.

For the next five years, he, Henry Justus, Joanie Walsh, and I worked together on making our business look more expensive than it ever would actually be by creating this incredible photography for both Van Heusen and Izod. We did photo shoots of Izod polar fleece products in snowstorms on the top of the mountain in Whistler in Vancouver, British Columbia. We shot in lakes in Big Bear, California; on glaciers in Alaska; on golf courses in Cabo; all over the world. We also played golf together, ate together, and spent a lot of time creating a vision for both brands: Van Heusen with the "Shirts for Men" campaign and Izod with "I Work. I Play. Izod." targeting sports enthusiasts.

During all this time, Mike proved to me that he was destined for a bigger role and belonged in our New York corporate headquarters.

In fact, by the time I left PVH, one of my proudest accomplishments was that Mike Kelly was one of the 26 people on my management team. Remember, he was working in a cubbyhole when I met him, and he'd come a long way from there to where he is now. I think he succeeded because he had all the necessary factors in place: I believe you have to be somewhat lucky, and he was. You have to put yourself in the right place, which he did. You have to have talent, and he had an enormous amount of talent. And you have to demonstrate that you can handle yourself well, and he did that repeatedly during the time we worked together on those photo shoots. I believe he did what needed to be done in front of the president of the company to get himself on that management council. If he hadn't, he might still be working in a division in a satellite office in New Jersey instead of for corporate in company headquarters in New York City.

My point in telling this story is that you never know who your next mentor is going to be or where you might meet that person. You need to always be prepared to put your best foot forward. When he first met me, Mike thought the purpose of our meeting was just to get my okay on joining the company. He had no idea—because I had no idea at that time—that meeting me would lead him to the executive suite of the largest men's shirt company in the world. Our meeting turned out to be the opportunity of a lifetime for him. It paid off for the company, too, because they would probably never have known what a creative, talented person they had working for them in a back-office job if we hadn't met that day and I hadn't seen his potential to do more at a much higher level of responsibility.

When I left PVH, one of the things I was most happy about was that I was able to help Mike, who needed a break, to train him and mentor him and ultimately put him on the executive committee. To this day, he's still there: he's one of the key people in charge of marketing. That meant a lot to me, and I'll bet it meant a lot to him, too.

Another person I mentored when he worked at DKI was Paul Kotrba. He was European and very worldly, he spoke three languages fluently, he was poised, and he carried himself extremely well. When I came to the company, he had a fairly high-level position in the United States and was doing just OK. As I've said before, though, my gray hair has given me some wisdom, and the more I watched him work, the more aware I became that he was not in tune at that time with the way we do business in this country. I didn't know why he was working sales in the United States when it seemed so obvious that with his background he should have been working in a sales capacity in the international division.

As I mentioned earlier, I'm not the type of person who starts cleaning house as soon as I take on a new responsibility, and so at first I simply asked his manager, President Mary Wang, "Don't you think he should be on the international side of the business?" Mary didn't want to move him at that time, and I respected that decision for a while. Finally, though, since I liked him and wanted him to succeed and since I get paid to make decisions, I decided to move him from the American side of the business to the international side.

> You never know who your next mentor is going to be or where you might meet that person. You need to always be prepared to put your best foot forward.

When I talked to Paul privately about my decision, he said, "I really appreciate that you're doing this, and I can't tell you how relieved I am. I believe I should have been on the international side of the business from the beginning. Now I can really focus on growing that business, and it's something I'm very comfortable with and familiar with."

As part of his new position, he needed to make presentations to the most senior managers in the company, and I noticed that he didn't seem to be as well liked by them as I had hoped. I asked some of my corporate counterparts what they thought of him, and I learned that they felt his information was not as thorough or specific as it should have been.

I still thought he had great potential. He was very young, and I felt he just needed to be taught what he had to know to succeed. He needed training, just as I had 30 years earlier. Although he reported to someone else in the company, I met with Mary and said I wanted to mentor him. She agreed to that arrangement, and I began to work very closely with him. I knew what questions to ask to force him to be more thorough and to drill down. For the next five years he partnered with me on every deal that we made in Asia or in Europe, and with Mary, of course, I've never seen anyone grow as much and as rapidly as Paul did just by having access to the senior management of the company and being able to dialogue directly with me. Corporate now looks at him as one of the lead players for the future, because he's still smart and sophisticated and he's been mentored and trained in the proper way.

In life, part of success is luck (you need to put yourself in a position to find luck) and part is understanding who you are and what you're capable of. I believe, as you now know, that there are no flukes in business: the cream rises to the top. People get to where they are because they deserve to be there, and I believe natural selection happens. When someone is not able to do a particular job, that person gets weeded out. I really believe the system works. If you have talent it needs to be honed and recognized.

39

Don't Forget to Thank People Who Help You

Naturally, if you mentor or help enough people, you're bound to find one or two who don't appreciate what you've done for them. That happened to me at least once during my career, and I tell this story as a cautionary tale to you, my readers, so you'll know what not to do when someone helps you get a job or a promotion.

I met this person—we'll call him Terry—many years ago. I signed a license with him, and as we continued to do business together, I got along well with him. In addition, I admired the fact that he was an entrepreneur: I've always respected entrepreneurs who risk their own money rather than risking other people's money.

Terry had a sizable business, which he operated on his own. He had what I call a one-foot kick: he sourced, bought, designed, and sold products. He had some help, but essentially he was running his own business. Eventually, Terry decided to sell his business to another company, whose owner called to ask me about Terry because they were discussing keeping him on to manage the business, and I gave him a good reference. The company bought Terry's business, but three months later I heard that Terry was gone. For whatever reason, the arrangement didn't work out.

Soon after that, Terry called and asked if he could meet with me. I said yes and asked him to tell me what had happened. He gave me his side of the story. Naturally, I checked out the other side of the story— as the saying goes, there are three sides to every story: yours, the other person's, and the truth—and whatever the truth was, I'll probably never know. Eventually, Terry got around to the point of this meeting and asked me if I could help him find another job. I didn't have anything at my company, but I did give him advice and recommendations for people he could call. I spoke on his behalf, and I conducted practice interviews with him. Because he could be abrasive at times, I schooled him on what to say and what not to say in a job interview as well as how to present himself. I spent a tremendous amount of time with him, as much time as he needed, which was sometimes twice a week for several months, both in person and on the phone. I was his sounding board as well as his best reference because I had a fancy title. Then I didn't hear from him for a while.

A month later I found out he had found a job. I didn't find that out from him, though; I heard it from a mutual friend. In fact, Terry never called to thank me or even to let me know he had gotten a job. Frankly, I think after all the time and effort I put in, I deserved at least a phone call to let me know he had gotten a job.

Anyway, a year later something went wrong at his new company, and lo and behold, Terry called again to ask if I could help him. I took his call and never said a word about not hearing from him a year earlier. Some people might think I should have let him know that he had behaved badly, but I believe there are certain lessons that people should be taught and there are certain lessons that their parents should have taught them. It wasn't up to me to let him know what I thought he should have done.

I'm including this example of how mentoring is often a one-way street to let you know—if you don't already—that you shouldn't burn bridges and should appreciate what people do for you. In my case, I don't regret the time I spent trying to help this person even though he didn't have the decency to keep me in the loop. I just let it go. But I'm human; I'm not sure I would put the interest and time in the next time.

40

It Pays to
Have Friends

DKI signed a license with a company named Marchpole, which had gone bankrupt for several reasons that had nothing to do with the business in which we were involved. We had granted them a global license for menswear, working with the CEO, Michael Morris. After about a year we started to sense that there were problems, but I didn't know how severe the problems were until I got a call that the company was going to declare bankruptcy.

Over the course of this period I had become very fond of Michael. He was smart, adventurous, and fun to be with, although in my view he took too many business risks and didn't appear to be interested in anyone else's opinion. However, he did know what he was doing.

The company was based in London, and so our New York lawyers coordinated for me to meet with a barrister for bankruptcy and arbitration procedures in England. A few days went by, and we started getting more concerned, because the company going into bankruptcy was at a point at which it would have to stop all shipments to our retail partners. Additionally, our revenues were at risk. However, when I first met Michael, he was capable but "fast and furious," so I decided to protect our company with a series of irrevocable LCs (letters of credit, which are guaranteed bank payments). It was clear to me that this business was in real trouble, and since it was affecting my business, I needed to know whether it could go forward. What could we do to not interrupt shipments?

I called Michael, who made it clear that he wanted to continue doing business with us after he went bankrupt. If he found new financial backers to help him resolve his financial issues, would I continue with him? He admitted that business would be difficult for him (and us and his other customers) until he got back on his feet, but he was confident that he would be back in business in relatively short order if I could help and allow him to find a new backer.

Meanwhile, my lawyer found out that the mediator had been approached by a company representing the Swiss pension fund, which was in partnership with a small company in London. They wanted to meet me to present their case for continuation. Two days later I went to London and met with our solicitor, who told me clearly that I had total control in this matter: because the company that declared bankruptcy had not paid us immediately what it owed us, the brand (which we owned) would revert back to our company 100 percent. This happened because of the way the deal had been structured: Lynn Usdan, our general counsel, and Tisha Kalberer, our CFO, are first rate. I had been concerned about this company from the outset, and so I had arranged to have $6.25 million in letters of credit guaranteed to my company in case there was a financial problem. In short, my solicitor explained, we were within our rights and there was no need to negotiate anything.

Then I met with the arbitrator, who echoed what my solicitor had said: "It's your decision. We'd like to call a meeting for this evening. That's why we asked you to come out here. You have a choice to listen to what the banks have to say. There are three different banks representing these letters of credit. We'd like you to listen to what they have to say, and in this case I'm on your side, because you have the rights here, and I want to support you in whatever you need."

That afternoon, armed with this knowledge, I met with the company representing the operating company and the Swiss pension fund, which had invested in Marchpole. They showed me their plan for how to go forward. They also asked me to look at the operating company that would continue to run this company on their behalf if I chose to do that. When I met the players, I was totally underwhelmed. In my view they didn't have the wherewithal or the experience to do what was necessary. They had never represented a designer global sportswear brand.

I did like Michael Morris and believed in his ability. He had made a mistake in overextending himself, but I trusted that he understood the business. That was why we gave him the license in the first place, and I knew he had everything he needed to rebound from bankruptcy. He soared too high, he made mistakes, and he needed to come down to earth, but I was committed to going forward with him because I believed in him.

Here's where the story gets interesting. At 8 p.m. I went into a paneled boardroom that had been set up by the arbitrator in the offices of one of the big banks in the London financial district. I sat at the end of a huge conference table. Sitting around the table were the arbitrator, 20 people from various different banks, and my lawyer. The banks began by asking me whether I would consider terminating the CEO who was currently operating the business (Michael), taking on a new partner in the name of this small company that was also backed by the Swiss pension fund (in addition to the banks), and forgoing my rights to the $6.25 million.

I looked around the table and said, "If I knew you were going to ask me for the $6.25 million, I would have told all of you to fly to New York instead of having me fly to London." I was being a wise guy when I said that, but I thought it was very funny. I'm from Brooklyn, and 20 bankers from some of the biggest banks in the world were asking me for money that I had no reason to give them. Stupid question. I don't believe LVMH ever understood how I protected the company and how clever (if I do say so myself) I was in structuring this deal and collecting the money.

In this case—as in many others in my career—it paid for Michael to have good friends and for me to be a good friend. I walked out happy, and the company that was going through bankruptcy recovered: he found new backers for his business, I supported him while he got back on his feet, and we continue to do business to this day. I had protected my company's interest two years earlier when I first negotiated this deal, and so I had all the leverage in this so-called negotiation. We collected $6.25 million for our troubles. As I've said before, the only argument I ever want to get in is one in which the other guy's in an indefensible position. In this case I couldn't lose. They couldn't defend their position. The key to negotiating is understanding who has the leverage and knowing when you have power and when you don't. I knew I had all the leverage.

The following day I went to see Michael. I told him what had occurred, I gave him a window of time to resurface with a legitimate partner, and finally told him I knew he wouldn't let me down. Friends. Oh yes, one more thing. Michael was now behind his desk and I asked him for a pen and paper. On it I wrote a note, folded it, and told him to put it in his wallet . . . "Thank G-d for Mark Weber." It's still in his wallet.

41

My Friend Bill

I was participating in a Van Heusen global conference in South Beach, Miami. I was having lunch with many of our associates when this handsome guy came over to our table. He had long hair that was silver white, not gray, and he reintroduced himself: "Hi, Mark. I'm Bill Montooth, your licensee for belts and small leather goods." I didn't remember him, but I asked him to join us at our table for lunch. Among other topics, we started talking golf. I had recently taken up the game, which was a passion for him. His handicap was 11, which made him somewhat accomplished. We talked on and on, then we discussed business.

Bill was vice president for Custom Leather Canada, and it became clear to me that he was a seasoned selling pro. His knowledge of the market—where the opportunities were and who were the decision makers on men's accessories—was insightful and very different in perspective from my view. He understood all channels of business and sold successfully into them. We started to discuss fashion. Like me, he was really interested in men's clothing: suits, shirts, and suede shoes (my personal favorite fashion item). It was kismet. We talked the same language. He was from Columbus, Ohio; by now, you know I'm from New York, so we were different but equal (that may be a little corny, but it's how I feel). I liked this guy.

Over the next few months I met Bill in our offices a few times, and we talked about fashion, business, and golf. As luck would have it, we were both scheduled to be at a conference, and we agreed that on the free day we would play golf together. I was really excited: here I had met a guy from the industry who had a high "cool" factor, and now we were to compete in golf.

A group of our guys and gals went to the Doral in Miami, a great golf facility now managed and owned by the Trump Organization. We started to play. Bill was strong and consistent; I was a mess and embarrassed. At the end of seven holes, I was tracking very poorly. I did par 8 and 9 and finished with a 50, Bill with a 44. Golf is a strange game: you can move your hands and grip only a quarter of an inch and go from horrible to champion.

But something clicked on the eighth hole and continued to go well. By the time we finished the seventeenth hole, I was in the hunt. The eighteenth hole is on an island green: the hole and flag are surrounded by water. I hit a good drive on a long par 4, hit a decent lie, and left myself 190 yards from the hole. Not an easy shot but makeable. I took out my 7 wood, which I had in my bag at the time, and put the ball ten feet from the hole and parred it for a 39 on the back nine. Bill shot a 46. I beat him by 1 stroke: 89 to 90.

That began one of the most, if not the most, important friendships in my life. First of all, I beat him, so the challenges were set for the future. I have beaten him good at some important tournaments, but I must admit he is better than I am and wins more often. There, I said it: Are you satisfied, Bill?

But even more important, Bill and I have enjoyed an amazing time together. Fashion and style, golf, and different skill sets. Forget that he is a great friend; he is my most important advisor in business. He is an amazing seller; people like him and trust him. He too has a creative side, and it supports his selling expertise.

Although we have traveled the world together, shopping and playing golf, his counsel is what I appreciate most. He was my closest and most treasured supporter when I left PVH. I trusted and still trust his judgment. He is from the Midwest, and maybe that's why he is so well balanced in business and in life. He can identify what's important. His business sense is always right, and because he is close to his customers, his insight is always, well, insightful. He has an unusual perspective. I have discussed many, if not all, strategy decisions and retail perspectives with him, and always I learn and grow.

Here's the takeaway. No matter who you are, you need good counsel. It is important to have a network of people whom you can download to; you need objective people who will tell you when you're right and, even more important, when you're wrong. You must seek out information in disciplines you don't excel in or don't have access to. The information, perspective, details, and counsel you get give you a better understanding of the business and prepare you for decision making with your staff. At PVH, it was Bruce; at LVMH, it's Bill and my friend Gene—all of whom are older than I.

42

The View of the
Eiffel Tower

D uring my career I have received two awards from the fashion industry of which I'm very proud. The first was from the Fashion Institute of Technology, where I lectured to groups of students (from 100 to 300 at a time) several times each semester for five years. That work was very rewarding. As you start to mature in business, you want to make sure that you're teaching people and giving them opportunities for their futures. I did that for FIT, and they were kind enough to thank me and honor me as their Man of the Year for the work I had done. Jarrod made an incredible speech—laughs, no pauses, expertly crafted. Amazing! I followed. No one remembered a word I said. He was tougher to follow than Larry Phillips.

The second award was from the AAFA, the American Apparel & Footwear Association. This prestigious award is given to a number of institutions, for example, the best retail company, which was Nordstrom the year I was selected as their Man of the Year. The evening the AAFA gave me that award, it showed a video that had been prepared by the DKI marketing team to salute me and introduce the tribute I would be given. The video featured my colleagues and business associates, as well as my sons Jarrod and Jesse, giving their opinions of me. I was very moved by this tribute, and I'd like to share their comments and congratulations here:

- Jarrod Weber, attorney: "Hello, boys and girls. So what's this meeting about?" (This is what I ask at the beginning of every meeting.)
- Jason Binn, founder, *DuJour* magazine: "Mark is —"
- Jesse Weber, attorney: "Driven."

- Tisha Kalberer, chief financial officer, DKI: "Consistent."
- Veronique Gabai-Pinsky, global brand president, Estee Lauder Designer Fragrances: "Smart."
- Maurice Reznik, CEO, Maidenform: "Very self-confident."
- Jarrod Weber: "Honest."
- Michael Morris, CEO, SK International/DKNY Menswear: "Cautious."
- Avril Oates, creative director, Galeries Lafayette: "Motivational."
- Hans Dorsinville, executive vice president and senior creative director, Laird + Partners: "Complex."
- Steve Grapstein, CEO, Como Holdings: "One of the more creative people I've ever met."
- Bill Montooth, vice president, Custom Leather USA: "A gentleman."
- Trey Laird, chief executive and creative officer, Laird + Partners: "Extremely detailed."
- Jason Binn: "Micro but macro."
- Mary Wang, president, DKNY: "And wants to win every day."
- Bono, lead singer of U2 and cofounder of EDUN: "What a man! What hair!"
- Steve Grapstein: "Mark, he has a vision. He knows what he's trying to create and what's best for the company."
- Michael Morris: "He was brought up in the men's business and understands product, production, and fabric and put it into the women's collections."
- Steve Grapstein: "It always amazes me how far you've taken the Donna Karan Group."
- Ronny Wurtzburger, president, Peerless Clothing: "He's a quick learner. He knows his competition. He studies them."
- Veronique Gabai-Pinsky: "Mark is a no-nonsense man."
- Mary Wang: "He is a bottom-line-driven individual."
- Trey Laird: "He's got a great eye, thinks like a merchant, and has a real passion for product."
- Karen Katz, president and CEO, Neiman-Marcus: "Mark is great at developing relationships."
- Maurice Reznik: "He wants to surround himself with people who share the passion for growth and success that he does."

- Jonathan Heilbron, president/CFO, Thomas Pink: "He gets people to want to work with him."
- Hans Dorsinville: "He's my creative collaborator."
- Steve Grapstein: "He put the logo everywhere, in places that probably we never even thought of before, helping to elevate the brand worldwide."
- Michael Morris: "All the time he gets, in his free time, he spends with his family."
- Bill Montooth: "He is passionate about life."
- Jesse Weber: "A really good role model for both Jarrod and me, socially and professionally."
- Jarrod Weber: "No matter how busy he was, he was always there for us. He's the greatest when it comes to family."
- Donna Karan, founder and creative director, DKI: "Hi, Mark. I want to congratulate you on winning this award tonight. You have really been committed to this industry, and I'm so glad we're celebrating your hard work, your energy, and your passion."
- Peter Hunsinger, then-publisher of *GQ,* now publisher of *Golf World* magazine: "Hey, Mark, congratulations. Bully for you."
- Avril Oates: "Congratulations, Mark."
- Jonathan Heilbron: "Many congratulations."
- Bono: "Congratulations, Mark."
- Tisha Kalberer: "You deserve it."
- Maurice Reznik: "You're the man."
- Hans Dorsinville: "You are a 10."
- Jesse Weber: "Really, really proud of you. We're very happy to share this moment with you."
- Donna Karan: "Thank you for joining our team, and thank you for all the hard work that you do, day in and day out, for us."

In the video, I had the last word: the team included a quote I had borrowed from James Carville and had mentioned in a prior speech I'd given: "I've had a remarkable experience at this company. You know, the company pays me for my mind; I've thrown in my heart for free. I like it here."

After the video, Antonio Belloni, the managing director of LVMH, went up to the podium to present me with the award. He had flown in from France for the occasion. He introduced me by referring to the videotape: "I am glad Mark threw in his heart for free, because his head was expensive enough." Everything in his address was moving and proved what I referred to earlier: I now had membership in this great French company, and even more important, I had their trust. I was moved by Toni's presentation, and I think the speech I gave on that memorable evening sums up how I feel about my entire career:

> Our industry—fashion, luxury—is often very much maligned. We sometimes forget what an amazing industry we're a part of. You know, we represent clothing, one of the five essentials necessary to sustain life. All you college grads out here, do you remember the other four? Think about it. Our industry employs millions of people all over the world, and we support families and their survival all over the world, and very often the third world's first industry to be born is textiles and apparel, which we should all be very proud of.
>
> And while we don't cure disease, our industry is one of the most benevolent and generous industries, as demonstrated right here tonight. I'm very proud to be part of the American Image Awards. For me, instantly, the need to think about what my American image would be the day I joined LVMH changed dramatically. I went from being an executive representing an American company to an American executive, and I can't tell you how important that was to me and how much time I put into thinking what goals, what positions, what should be important to me as I faced a new group, the LVMH group.
>
> You know, as my hair starts to get gray, I like to think that I've gained some wisdom, and perhaps the fact that, you know, I was a little over 40, and being involved with this group was so significant, maybe, maybe that wisdom helped me position myself. I can tell you, believe it or not, I was not interested in money. I was not interested in titles. I was not interested in power, nor was I interested in corporate politics. I had been there, and I had done that, and Toni, thank you for that comment about my income: you should know I would have worked for free.
>
> I wanted to be a solid citizen. I wanted to be the kind of person—an American person in a European company—that could be respected, honored, and trusted, and that's where I put my drive. I dedicated myself to trying to do the best I could to deliver

on a promise of Donna Karan International within the LVMH stable. While Toni mentioned some of my other responsibilities, and I really appreciate him recognizing it, there was nothing more important to me in my business life than to deliver on the promise of Donna Karan, one of the world's great brands.

LVMH made the decision to make that part of their group, and for whatever the reasons were, they were unsuccessful in delivering on the financial goals. I was so motivated by that, and I came to the company, new CEO, all people in place, and I was *shocked* to find out what a talented group of people were working with Donna, and to this day, all the direct reports, all the senior management at Donna Karan are still there. Donna Karan, the person, built an extraordinary company with extraordinary individuals; what they needed were some rules and some discipline. And frankly, when people ask me, they come up and say it, I don't know whether I'm smart, that's for someone else to determine, but I am convinced I'm well-trained, and I've been very, very fortunate to have gone through that kind of training.

When you think about being an American in a European company, you have to consider so many different things. I was hopeful, and I suppose tonight hearing Toni say what he said, confident now that I made my mark in the way I wanted to. I have always believed that if you put the company first and treat a company fairly, it will come back and pay you in spades, and I was very happy about that, and I'm really, really very fortunate to be part of this group.

I must say that being part of a team where the senior management is based 4,000 miles away, there are language barriers, there are difficult differences in culture, and it is lonely at times, and it is foreign, and I have found over time that it requires reflection, and in life and careers there's some very, very special moments, and I would like to share one of those moments with you.

I was in Paris for a strategic planning meeting with LVMH. We were about to present our strategic plans for the next three years, and as I walked down the Avenue Montaigne toward the LVMH headquarters, it was early, the dew was coming off the ground, and I remember the feeling I had of being part of this. I went up to the boardroom floor. I was the first there. The boardroom was dark, the shades were down, and I pressed the lights on, and I pressed the button, and as the shades came up, the sun shone in, and I was looking out at the Eiffel Tower, and I must admit that seeing that and realizing what I had become a part of, tears came to my eyes. I thought about the fact that I did okay for a kid from Brooklyn, and I'm a long way from Madison Avenue.*

I have been very fortunate. I've had a stellar career. I walked the Great Wall of China when I was younger than my children. I've written a book. I've had more jobs and more responsibilities, more promotions than anyone could imagine to have. I've been very fortunate. I've had so many special moments, but tonight is one of the most special ones of my life and my career, and I would like to tell you why.

When I was 26 years old, I was invited to my first American Image Awards, and I'll never forget how new, how exciting, and how special that felt: all the celebrities, all the powerful industry people, government officials, it was amazing. It was bigger than life. It was a "wow!" I was mesmerized, and I'll never forget, the ceremony began, and I was holding my wife Susie's hand, and I was in awe. I remember leaning over and I said to her, "What do you think you have to do to get one of those awards?" Susie looked at me, she smiled, she squeezed my hand, and she said, "You'll figure it out." So Susie, it took quite some time. But you were right: I figured it out.

---

*Madison Avenue is where PVH's offices were located.

43

Just in Case You Weren't Paying Attention . . .

Finally, I'd like to recap some of the lessons in this book that I've lived by and that I believe can help others—I mean *you*—succeed in business and in life:

1. Creativity without knowledge and business skills is very limiting. Learn as much as you can about every aspect of the business and industry you're in.
2. Work is work if it's work. If you love what you're doing, you're going to love your career. Find something you're really passionate about doing and don't be afraid to make a change if you don't love what you start out doing.
3. You're not supposed to know what to do with your life when you're starting out. Yes, some people do (or at least have some idea), and if you do, more power to you. The rest of you will reach your destiny by accident, as I did, and that can lead to success too.
4. You don't have to come from money or have connections or go to the best schools to succeed in your career. But you do need to figure out what's special about you and find a business that will appreciate that skill or talent or quality.
5. Be open to mentors wherever they present themselves. I firmly believe that you should always answer when opportunity knocks because you never know what or who is on the other side of that door.

6. When you're interviewing for a job, you need to work hard to understand who you're going to be meeting with and what might be important to that person.

7. Don't choose or accept a job just because it pays well: money should not be the deciding factor. There are other, more important factors that should inform your decision: the company, your manager, your coworkers, whether you'll be trained and have an opportunity to learn, and the potential for career advancement.

8. Make sure the people you work with are helping you learn and advance in your job and the company. If they're not, recognize that this job is just one rung on your ladder and start planning your next move—at another company.

9. When you're young, recognize that youth is on your side: you are the future of your company and your business. Youth is something older executives covet because you know more than you think you do.

10. Decide what you really want from your career. Do you want to be a puppet, or do you want to be the puppet master, the person who pulls the strings? If it is the latter, keep in mind that you need to get interested in things that may not interest you; you don't need to be proficient in everything, but you do need to learn all you can about as much as you can.

11. Ask not what your company can do for you; ask what you can do for your company. If you help your company and do the right thing, your company will help you and do right by you too.

12. Show your boss and the people around you that no task is too big or too small for you, that you are the go-to person they need. Even if you don't know how to do something, you have to be seen as someone who is smart enough to figure out whom to talk to and find someone who can help you. Make sure your managers know you're someone they can rely on to get the job done.

13. Don't allow yourself to get stuck in a stovepipe where the only way to advance is straight up; that's too limiting. This is another reason you should learn as many other areas of your business as possible. Let people know you want to do more in other areas, because that's the best way to advance up the ladder.

14. Don't accept the norm, or "that's the way we've always done things." Instead, be a disruptor: find a more efficient or productive or direct way of doing something, and if it's good for your company—and if you present your case well—management will appreciate that you're looking out for them and coming up with new ideas.

15. Do what you're great at, not what you think you should do to move up. This world is competitive, and you're going to be competing with people who are the best at what they do, and so you need to be the best too.

16. Don't be a wise guy and learn to understand both the culture of your company and the cultures you're working with. Many other cultures are more reserved than Americans are, and you need to respect that—and them—if you're going to succeed, especially in international business.

17. Never compromise your integrity or yourself in any way. Remember, even the appearance of impropriety is problematic. Don't accept gifts of any kind from anyone, because when you do, that person owns you and will call in that favor at some future time.

18. The way you deal with disappointments, setbacks, mistakes, and failures is more important than the way you deal with success. Don't let your ego or sense of entitlement—or your emotions—get in your way. This is business, and your colleagues are not your friends or family. Be humble and work even harder to get what you want in your career. Let your disappointments fuel your desire to achieve.

19. Learn the financial side of your business: you can't get to the top without it even if you know everything else. Let your managers know that you want to learn more and ask them if they'll help you. If they won't, learn it on your own time, because you can't run a business if you don't understand how it makes money.

20. Know how to package and present yourself. This means you first need to know how to dress appropriately for the business you're in. Second, learn how to prepare well-organized, detailed presentations and how to deliver them confidently to large groups of people.

21. Follow your instincts but back them up with facts. If you have a new idea, have the courage of your convictions and present it

to your managers but make sure you can support it with solid factual details.

22. Make deals and partnerships only if you're sure they're right for your company. Don't let your emotions get in the way; don't become blinded by the desire to do something. Sometimes the right answer is no, and sometimes the best deal is the one you walk away from.

23. If you're up against strong competition, find an unconventional way to compete. Zig when the rest of your industry is zagging; do something counterintuitive and you may be surprised by the successful results.

24. Be open to meeting anyone and everyone you can because you never know how those relationships may pay off either in financial terms or in friendship; both are equally valuable. Go out of your way to help others because that also benefits you in the long run.

25. Count your blessings—even if you're terminated. Celebrate your successes and recognize that even though your company has taken your job, it can't take away your skills. There is a new and exciting opportunity out there if you plan properly.

26. Bear in mind George Patton's words: "The test of success is not what you do when you are on top. Success is how high you bounce back when you hit the bottom." If you lose a job or face some other setback, don't let anyone grind you down; work harder and smarter to climb back up. Call everyone you know to see if anyone can help you and don't take the first thing that comes along. Instead, wait for the right position for you.

27. When you're looking for a new position, don't think only about the companies you want to work for; in addition; think about what companies need your background, experience, and know-how.

28. Looking for a new job is a complicated, painful process, and it's very easy to lose confidence in yourself. Fight that tendency: don't forget who you are and how competent, skilled, talented, and experienced you are. This is another time in your life when you know more than you think you do; don't let anyone tell you different.

29. When you're between jobs, you should be willing to recalibrate in terms of what you're earning or your job responsibilities or

your title or position. That doesn't mean you will accept less, but you have to be willing to. Don't let your ego get in your way.

30. Don't let anyone in business push you around: if you're well trained and know your business, your track record will speak for itself.

31. Keep in mind that managing is a multidirectional process. You need to manage up to your bosses, down to your staff, sideways to your colleagues, and outward to your partners, vendors, suppliers, and customers.

32. Love the one you're with unless there's a good reason not to. Don't replace people just for the sake of having someone new or because you want your own people. Instead, take the time to find out why they haven't been successful yet, and if you can fix that problem, you may not need to replace anyone at all.

33. Never forget that you're in business to make money. Yes, there are other reasons as well, but if you don't make money, you can't achieve any other goals. Set appropriate financial goals and do everything you can to meet the projections you set.

34. Find partners who believe in your vision and share your goals. This is extraordinarily important in working with licensees, but it's also critical in every aspect of business. Don't settle for good enough because that isn't good enough.

35. Behind anyone with vision, there are 50 well-intentioned people undermining that vision. Don't let them get in your way if you can prevent it. My favorite word is "no" because it opens up so many doors, so many ways to think creatively about how to turn that "no" into a "yes." Don't take no for an answer (if you have the data to back you up): you need to have the stamina, willpower, and drive to persuade people and fight for what you know is the right thing to do.

36. Developing new ideas is what drives the fashion business. If you work in this industry, you need to recognize that your company or your products need to always strive to be different. No one needs new fashions; it's our job to create products that people want.

37. The fashion business is all about product. You can run from product, but you can't hide: sooner or later you need to understand what makes a good product.

38. There's no substitute for good taste in any business, not only fashion. If you don't know the difference between good and great, you don't belong in the fashion business.

39. We now live and work in an instantaneous global society, and if you want to compete in that world, you must think globally and develop a product line that works around the world. Many companies make the mistake of thinking they need different product lines for different regions, and ultimately that hurts them; don't make that mistake in your business.

40. You can have whatever point of view you want; it's how you express your viewpoint that matters. Don't get excited or angry or scream at people. People in business want to see you as someone who understands what the important issues are and who can handle problems while maintaining control.

41. When you're interviewing someone for a job, know what you can and can't ask to avoid getting into legal hot water. Learn how to interview well, because hiring the wrong person is bad for both of you: remember, you're playing with someone's life.

42. As you climb the ladder to success, try to help others climb it too. Mentoring is important both when you're working your way up (as a recipient) and when you've achieved enough that you can become a mentor and share your knowledge, training, and experience with more junior people.

43. Don't forget to thank anyone and everyone who helps you in business (and in life). Don't burn your bridges by being careless or thoughtless: follow up.

44. Take time to appreciate what you've achieved in your life and career. The hardest math you can master is learning how to count your blessings, and it's important to do that.

45. Be considerate of others: it brings rewards far greater than any you can achieve in business. It's the right thing to do and the best way to live.

MY JOB HIERARCHY

Assistant Designer
Designer, Knitwear, Boys
Designer, Boys' Collections
Men's Sportswear Designer
Men's Fashion Director Dress Shirts
Men's Fashion Director and Marketing Director
Men's VP Merchandising Dress Shirts
Senior VP, Menswear
Executive VP, Menswear
Executive VP, Menswear and Private Label
President, Men's Dress Shirts
President, Van Heusen Company
Corporate Vice President, Product Development/
    Marketing
President, Phillips-Van Heusen International
President of International and the Van Heusen Company
Vice Chairman, Sportswear
Vice Chairman, Sportswear and G.H. Bass
President, Phillips-Van Heusen Corporation
Elected to Board of Directors
CEO, Phillips-Van Heusen
CEO, LVMH Inc.
Member Executive Committee, LVMH
Chairman/CEO, Donna Karan
Operational Corporate Oversight, Thomas Pink
Operational Corporate Oversight and Member of
    the Board, EDUN
Mark Weber Advisory Group LLC
Consultant to M3 Relativity/Relativity Media

ACKNOWLEDGMENTS

I have so many people to thank. First and foremost, my father-in-law, Joe Koperwas, who after my marriage told me never to make decisions out of fear for money because he would "have my back," and to him and Regina, his wife, for Susie.

To my wife, Susie, who has been the brains of this "outfit" and is always cool, calm, and measured under fire.

My unending thanks to my two boys, Jarrod and Jesse, both accomplished attorneys, who keep me young, still seek my counsel, and provide the drive to compete against them at golf as if I were a 21-year-old kid.

A special thank-you to Jarrod (and Ina, our newest family addition), who suggested that my stories were interesting enough to share with others. He arranged the first meeting with McGraw-Hill.

I have had a number of important mentors, none more important than Bruce Klatsky, without whom I would never have come this far.

To PVH for the beginning and the strength they inadvertently fueled when I left.

Thank you, LVMH, for the chance at an exciting second chapter in my career. Particularly Bernard Arnault for inspiration, Toni Belloni for leadership, Madame Concetta Lanciaux for the sign-off, Edie Steinberg for putting me through, and Chantal Gaemperle for the support. I have enjoyed being an American individualist in a French luxury company.

Donna Karan, Picasso with fabric.

A special callout to all those individuals with whom I worked inside and outside my companies. You demanded the best I could give.

Thank you to the people in our industry, the retail and luxury sectors all around the globe. You deserve a safe, prosperous, and healthy environment: the industry is trying.

Thank you to Judy Lugo, my assistant from the beginning.

Thank you to Mary Glenn of McGraw-Hill for having faith that my stories and experiences would be of interest to a broad cross section of people and to Ruth Mills for all her help and guidance in bringing my stories to these pages.

I'd also like to thank the motion picture industry for the inspiration it provided to a 12-year-old boy who was recovering at home from pneumonia for three months and watched every movie the TV had to offer. Those movies offered spectacular stories and lessons in life that provided inspiration and role models as well as a style to emulate.

And lastly, thank you, Brooklyn, New York. I wouldn't be this guy without having grown up in your streets.

Remember: there is no substitute for good taste.

INDEX

Charity events, 80–81
Chirico, Manny, 88, 96
Cohen, Patti, 126, 160
Communication, professional, 181
Companies:
    changing, 27–28, 58
    exploring other, 126
Compensation, 95–96, 119–120
Competition, 40–41, 209, 210
Confidence, 116, 118, 121, 210
Considerate, being, 212
Contacts:
    being open to new, 8, 89–92, 210
    in job searches, 105–108, 122
    value of, 195–197
Contribution(s):
    to company's success, 23–26, 208
    identifying companies that need
        your, 114, 210
    by young people, 19–20, 208
Control, 21–22, 151–154, 208
Converters, textile, 34–37
Cooper, Alice, 80–82
Counsel, seeking, 199–200
Coworkers:
    disagreements with, 179–181
    earning respect of, 17
    learning from, 208
Creativity, xiii, 155, 207
Criticism, 171–174
Cross-channeling, 29–31
Crystal Brands Company, 75–79
Culture(s):
    within companies, 23–24, 26
    as concern in product development,
        177–178
    sensitivity to, 43–47, 209
Custom Leather Canada, 199
Customers:
    end users vs., 64–65
    wants vs. needs of, 167–168

D

Deals, walking away from, 75–78,
    210
Debates, 129–130
Decision making, 78, 136–137, 157,
    158
Departments, changing, 29–31

Designers, 170–174, 183
Dior, 132
Disagreements, 97, 123–132, 179–181
Disappointment, 49–53, 209
Discipline, leadership and, 146–148
Discipline(s), business:
    learning about other, 21–22, 41,
        55–58
    promotions based on excellence in,
        39–41
Disrupting systems, 33–37, 209
DKI (see Donna Karan International)
DKNY Artworks, 160
DKNY brand, 114, 115, 129, 151, 153,
    155–160, 174
DKNY Jeans, 115, 129
Donna Karan Collection, 115, 129,
    174
Donna Karan International (DKI),
    xv
    global expansion of, 175
    goals at, 146–148
    inventory management and
        shipping at, 149–150
    job interviews at, 114–119,
        123–132
    mentoring at, 190–192
    Paris trip for, 141
    press coverage of interview at,
        133–135
    reputation of, 28
    Gene Rothkopf's work for, 91
Dorsinville, Hans, 160, 202, 203
Douglas, Michael, 82
Downs, Marcia, 37

E

EDUN, 213
Egypt, ancient, xi
Emotions:
    controlling, 51, 52, 179–181, 212
    in decision making, 78
End users, customers vs., 64–65
Energy, 55–58
Entourage (television series), 107, 108
Entry-level jobs, 11–12
European markets, 176–177
Expectations, recalibrating, 122
Experience, lack of, 19–20

ABOUT THE AUTHOR

Mark Weber began his career at the publicly-traded Phillips-Van Heusen Corporation (PVH), becoming president, board member, and CEO. He joined Louis Vuitton Moët Hennessy (LVMH) in 2006 as CEO LVMH Inc. (USA) and chairman and CEO of Donna Karan International Inc., where he oversaw the brand's growth in products and distribution around the globe in markets such as China, India, the Mideast, and Europe.